HELEN
STEVENS

THE EMBROIDERER'S COUNTRYSIDE

THE
EMBROIDERER'S
COUNTRYSIDE

HELEN M. STEVENS

For my parents
Thanks for everything

Photography throughout by
Nigel Salmon, Fotofayre, Bury St Edmunds, Suffolk

A DAVID & CHARLES BOOK
Copyright © Helen M. Stevens 1992
First published 1992

Helen M. Stevens has asserted her right to be identified as author of this work in accordance with the Copyright, Designs and Patents Act 1988.
A catalogue record for this book is available from the British Library.

ISBN 0 7153 9945 4

Typeset by ICON, Exeter, Devon
and printed in Germany by Mohndruck GmbH
for David & Charles
Brunel House Newton Abbot Devon

CONTENTS

PREFACE

Artist, embroiderer, herbalist and countryman, St Dunstan (909-88) was, tradition says, seated in his cell at his embroidery frame when the Devil appeared to him. Satan tempted him with all the lures of worldly pleasures, but, unable to impress Dunstan, he finally began to threaten him with all the powers of darkness. In a pot on the rough wooden table, gathered that morning from the hedgerow, was a bunch of fragrant yellow St John's wort, a proof against all evil spells and curses. The Devil, furious at his impotence in the plant's presence, seized Dunstan's embroidery needle and plunged it repeatedly into the waxy green leaves, but to no avail. Its strength overcame him and he was forced to disappear in a cloud of foul smelling smoke. To this day the correct name for this common country plant is perforate St John's wort. When the leaves are held up to the light they reveal the tiny holes inflicted by Dunstan's embroidery needle.

◁ *PLATE 1*
Frontispiece. The woodland floor
14 x 15.5cm (5^{1}/2 x 6in)

INTRODUCTION

There I will make thee beds of roses
And a thousand fragrant posies,
A cap of flowers and a kirtle
Embroider'd all with leaves of myrtle.

'The Passionate Shepherd to his Love'
C. Marlowe

PLATE 2 >
The Wildflower Meadow. Modern farming
methods have meant the loss of many
traditional meadowlands with their teeming
insect and bird life. Embroidery is the ideal
medium in which to recapture those sunny
summer days where the perfect picnic site was
only ever a carefully closed gate away
24.25 x 29.25cm (9¹/2 x 11¹/2in)

For centuries the countryside has inspired artists and writers alike. It has been portrayed and interpreted through every medium, sometimes stylised out of all recognition, sometimes romanticised until much of its raw beauty and strength has been lost, but textile art and the natural world have always enjoyed a special relationship, drawn together by the threads of tradition.

Embroidery forms an integral part of many country customs and much folklore, but as areas of our countryside disappear for ever beneath motorways, factories and the ever present need for housing, the strands linking us to this natural heritage of inspiration are often severed. We are fortunate, however, that all has not been lost. There still remain rare and precious stretches of medieval, even Anglo-Saxon, hedgerow, small acreages of ancient woodland, lovingly preserved expanses of virgin heathland and peaceful strips of fen and riverside, as well as rolling arable farmland, grazing downs, highlands, hills and forestry plantations.

Fig 1 >
Czechoslovakian folk motifs showing chickens
and a corn stook are typical of the folk
embroidery of Eastern Europe, which has
counterparts in most national costumes

. . . .

The countryside is still an inspiration in terms of embroidery.

There are many parallels between the natural world and embroidery. Just as a single stitch on the canvas is meaningless, so every species depends upon its neighbours to thrive and survive. Plants need insects to pollinate their flowers, insects and animals need plants for food and shelter. The food chain of plant, insect, bird, animal is a series of interconnected links, just as surely as a successful line of stem stitch is a series of interdependent but separate stitches.

PLATE 3 ▷
The smallest patio can become a microcosm of the countryside, and potted pelargoniums can attract unwanted visitors in the shape of greenfly. Placed in a secluded corner, however, even these apparently irksome residents can encourage more attractive guests in the shape of tiny, secretive wrens
(Troglodytes troglodytes)
11.25 x 16cm (4^1/$_4$ x 6^1/$_4$in)

Although the actual process of embroidery is more often than not undertaken in the protective womb of the studio or study, in fine weather the temptations of a clear blue sky and unadulterated daylight can lure the most spotlight-addicted embroiderer into the open air. The memory of the scratch of a bramble and the sound of birdsong will enhance the design process and bring a sharpness of recollection when embroidery is actually underway. In a rural setting, subjects are easy to find, but even in the city there is plenty of potential; less regimented gardens, parks, and even tubs and window boxes, yield rewards. Areas of wasteground, disused railways and cemeteries are often wildlife oases.

Advice to painters has often included the suggestion that they should try to see 'with the eyes of a child', capturing the wonder and enthusiasm so frequently lost as we grow up. Where watercolours demand that we should stand back fully to appreciate the skill of their working, embroidery invites both originator and subsequent viewer to do the opposite. Embroidery is an intimate art form, it draws its enthusiasts close and binds their attention with detail. To grasp the complexities of nature, perhaps we should abandon our everyday notions of perception, and rather put ourselves into a new dimension where small questing animals scurry feverishly through the undergrowth in the search for food, and where a bird's eyes are alert to the least movement of an insect, the tiniest vibration of a spider's web.

< PLATE 4
A balmy summer evening may find the day-flying spurge hawkmoth (Hyles euphorbiae) *in the company of late pollen-hungry bees, and a sunny window box can bring nature almost within touching distance – certainly well within range of the sketch pad*
7.5 x 9cm (3 x 3¹/₂in)

PLATE 5 ▷
The shamrock of Ireland and the English rose
intertwine to symbolise a marriage between
respective nationalities, and the red hips of the
wild rose add colour and drama to the design.
The traditional language of flowers can
add another dimension to the enjoyment of
countryside subjects
21.5 x 10.25cm (8¹/₂ x 4in)

< *Fig 2*
The floral symbols of the United Kingdom

Time-lapse photography has revealed many of the secrets of this 'other world' and freeze-frame techniques have held an instant of time motionless. But such mechanical devices, brilliant though their results may be, can only tell half the story. With the main subject in focus the background recedes; throw the setting into relief and the foreground loses its outline. In embroidery, all features can coexist. The quiver of a mouse's whiskers can disappear behind and emerge from the curl of a dead leaf. The green-gold tendril of a vine can interweave stems and grasses either as a backdrop or as a half-veiling screen, bringing the main subject of the picture into prominence with neither loss of reality nor detail.

If such studies of the natural world are to be made convincing, however, and to have relevance at a time when we are becoming increasingly aware of the specific interdependence of species upon one another, it is necessary to have some knowledge of how various species coexist. A thing of beauty may be a joy for ever, but it can also be an embarrassment should the subject matter go badly awry. It is a nonsense to picture a butterfly heading blissfully towards a food plant which is anathema to its tastes, although there is a place for symbolism where it is clearly evident as such. The juxtaposition of a rose, daffodil, thistle and shamrock, which all bloom at different times of the year is unrealistic, but as a visual euphemism for the United Kingdom it is delightful.

Fig 3 ▷
The common mallow sketched as a preliminary
to preparing a full embroidery design

Much can be learned from the study of good wildlife handbooks, but there is no substitute for personal observation and a notebook and sketch pad containing ideas jotted down during country walks or relaxed afternoons in your own back garden or patio. Try not to be afraid of making rough sketches, however basic, to remind you of what you may see. They can always be re-drawn with a little judicious reference to their exact shape and size in textbooks. Without some kind of aide-memoire it is difficult to recall which plants you may have seen growing together or the patterns into which autumn leaves may have fallen which so appealed to you at the time. Many of the rough sketches in this book which show subjects from different angles and perspectives have acted as source material for the embroideries themselves. They serve as catalysts rather than drawings in their own right.

Unless you are absolutely sure that a plant is so common as to be entirely unexceptional never pick it, however tempted you may be to take home a live specimen. A friend once remarked to George Bernard Shaw that he was surprised never to see flowers in the old man's house, knowing how fond he was of them. Shaw replied that he was fond of children, but did not have their heads lopped off to decorate his study. In any case, a wildflower brought into captivity immediately loses its chief appeal – that of its natural surroundings. It is better to observe, note and sketch, and your confidence will soon be boosted as your jotter fills up.

From the minutiae of hedgerow and woodland it is an intriguing leap to the broader canvas of full landscapes, but here too we must try to see through eyes other than our own. A kestrel hovering high above grassy plains can discern the furtive scampering of a mouse from a hundred feet, so it must also see the meadow flowers, May blossom in a distant hedge, the bright patches of autumn fruit and berries as the seasons turn. In the same way, the tiniest strategically placed

◁ *PLATE 6*
Spring gives way to summer. It is unlikely that
this scene would ever be glimpsed in actuality,
as the May blossom is usually long-fallen before
the foxgloves (Digitalis purpurea) *are open,*
but what better description could there be of a
fresh spring's melting into the warmth of
another summer? The lime hawkmoth
(Mimas tiliae) *flies both by day and night*
10.25 x 21.75cm (4 x 8¹/₂in)

Fig 4 △
*A rough landscape sketch need not include any
of the details of a finished embroidery, but will
serve as a reminder of a particular scene*

stitch, whilst seeming almost so small as to be insignificant, can draw the eye to a fulcrum in the picture and stimulate exploration of the whole landscape. Where close-up studies can only feature a few species at a time, wider landscapes can offer the opportunity to include a dozen or more varieties: banks of swaying loosestrife and willowherb, frothy masses of lacy cow parsley and tall spikes of mallow. Such combinations of detail and impressionism can create magical landscapes.

It cannot be purely coincidence that so many of our most expressive and flexible stitches arise directly from nature: stem, seed, seeding, fly, thorn, wheatear, and the most descriptive of all, feather stitch (the medieval *opus plumarium*, literally feather work). Feather stitch emulates the way in which feathers lie smoothly, yet with infinite changes of direction, upon a bird's body. It has evolved into today's familiar long-and-short and satin stitches. However, these stitches have become victims of their own success, in that the rules relating to their 'correct' application often restrict their flexibility.

PLATE 7 ▷
*The buddleia, or butterfly bush, flourishes on
many areas of wasteland, even in inner city
areas, and can be seen growing alongside old
brick walls (in summer massed with ragged
wallflowers) in railway shunting yards.
Apparently oblivious to their surroundings,
peacock butterflies (*Inachis io*) flock to
the bushes where they feed on nectar,
or bask open winged in the sunlight*
10.25 x 9cm (4 x 3½in)

This book is to some extent, a personal view of the countryside as reflected in the work of an individual artist. For country lovers who will see it simply as an interpretation of a much loved subject through an unusual medium, I hope it is visually exciting and thought provoking.

For embroiderers seeking fresh stimulus I have sought to offer both inspirational and practical advice. The advice and information may be sifted through, adapted or discarded to suit your own requirements. These pages should be about extending your own style, not sublimating it to another's.

PLATE 8 ▽

The Saxon Church. Nestling among summer foliage, the ivy-clad tower and red-tiled roof provides both challenge and inspiration to the embroiderer. With traditional techniques, straight stitching, seed stitch and a little impressionism, a warm afternoon in midsummer can be captured for ever
15.75 x 15.75cm (5³/4 x 5³/4in)

HELEN
STEVENS

CHAPTER ONE

SPRING HEDGEROW

Hark, where my blossomed pear tree in the hedge
Leans to the field and scatters on the clover
Blossoms and dewdrops — at the bent spray's edge.

'Home Thoughts from Abroad'
Robert Browning

THREADS DRAWN FROM LIFE

In early spring the first pin-pricks of green light appear to punch their way through the dark canvas of winter and the colourful fabric of the new year begins to unfold. We know that spring is coming, but still there is an element of suprise as the spiky branches of the hedgerow begin to flush with a hundred different shades of green. Later the blossoms appear, and beneath the hedgerow shrubs and trees the wildflowers burst into life.

During one of the first really warm days of April, when the sun had been hot enough to dry the puddles along the side of the country road, the notes were taken and the sketch made for the study shown in Plate 10. The cow parsley had barely broken out of its buds, its florets were still tightly curled, and the fragile stitchwort was clustered around the base of the taller plant. From a nearby holly hedge the first flight of holly blue butterflies had taken to the wing, still so recently hatched

Fig 5
Rough sketch for Plate 10

◁ PLATE 9

In spring the countryside comes to life in a burst of activity and life. The weasel (Mustela nivalis) *usually hunts at ground level, but in spring it will often climb high enough to take young birds from nests.*

The song thrush's (Turdus philomelos) *favourite food is snails, but with a hungry brood demanding attention earthworms are a welcome addition to the menu.*

Butterflies of the large-white family (Pieris brassicae) *are common in the spring. The pastel-coloured spring flowers which feature here are the bush vetch* (Vicia sepium), *cowslips* (Primula veris) *and the rare pasque flower* (Pulsatilla vulgaris). *Shrubs which blossom at the same time include the lesser pear* (Pyrus cordata) *and May* (Crataegus monogyna).
Embroidery shown life size:
41 x 24cm (16 x 9^1/2in)

PLATE 10 ▷

Queen Anne's lace is one of the more descriptive country names for cow parsley (Anthriscus sylvestris) *and its best known use has always been the making of pea-shooters from its tough, hollow stems.*

A preparation of the delicate stitchwort (Stellaria holostea), *boiled in wine with acorns was the standard remedy for a 'stitch'.*

The orange-tip butterfly (Anthocharis cardamines) *can be the bane of a vegetable gardener's life. A patient vigil beside a cabbage patch may well result in a sighting.*
Embroidery shown life size:
17.25 x 29.25cm (6^3/4 x 11^1/2in)

that the iridescent scales of their wings glittered like jewels while the papery wings of the orange tip beat more lazily. The tiny wings of the ladybirds whirred as they took short, halting flights from one plant to the next. Immediately the suggestion of the finished embroidery presented itself, but embroidery is not an art which allows instantaneous results. However, the mood had to be captured and the bare facts recorded: 'April 30th, budding cow parsley, greater stitchwort, holly blues, orange tip, ladybirds.' A scratchy sketch (Fig 5) served only to recall the gentle curve and branching of the cow parsley. It was enough to recapture that spring morning many months later when the fleeting scene had vanished for ever.

Once bitten by the bug of nature, it is difficult not to succumb to the heady temptation of cramming too much, too early, into every picture. First, there are rules to be learned, pitfalls to avoid and confidence to be gained. A simple study such as Plate 11 captures only a few square inches of the spring hedgerow, but nevertheless introduces several important ideas.

We take light for granted in the open air, but its presence and direction influences the appearance of everything we see, and because embroidery is not an instantaneous art, it is something which must be re-created at the very outset. Primroses are one of the earliest of spring flowers and their friendly, open faces make ideal subject matter for the novice sketcher (see Fig 6), but they can appear

PLATE 11 >

The word butterfly was probably first coined to describe the butter-coloured brimstone (Gonepteryx rhamni) *and was gradually expanded to cover the whole of the species. The present name brimstone relates to the colour of sulphur, with far less pleasant connotations.*

The brimstone is a powerful flyer, often covering many miles in a day and is a frequent visitor to wayside and woodland flowers. Unfortunately for would-be sketchers, it feeds for long periods with its wings closed before moving on to the next flower, but if you know brimstones are in your area it is often worth a wait beside any yellow flowers, as they often seem particularly attracted to these.

The common name for the primrose (Primula vulgaris) *comes from the Latin 'first roses'. The flowers were gathered by village maidens to decorate their dresses during spring festivals and are a symbol of purity. Simplified versions of the flowers are to be found among many folk embroidery patterns 9 x 9cm (3¹/₂ x 3¹/₂in)*

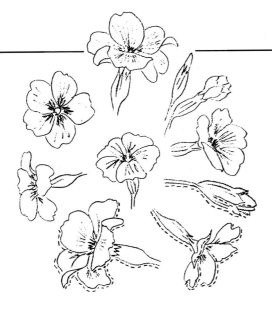

Primroses. The dotted lines on the three lower studies indicate which of the petal and sepal edges should be emphasised by a shadow line

flat and lifeless in embroidery unless a light source is implied. This is a rule which holds true in practically every case. Before you take your first stitch, imagine where the light is coming from inside your picture. If it is from the top right hand of your design, shadow the work with a fine line of black stem stitch along the bottom left-hand outline of each separate part of the picture. This may initially appear stark, but when disguised by the colour of the finished piece it will appear as a subtle shadow line to bring the subjects to life.

Everything about primroses speaks of beginnings, so they are an appropriate flower to choose for a first foray into *opus plumarium*. Their cheerful round faces are ideal subjects and the radial stitching used is a primary technique (see Fig 7). As already mentioned, *opus plumarium* literally translates as 'feather work' and as such needs little explanation. Next time you find the feather of a large bird, examine it closely and you will see how the web of its filaments lies together smoothly, only subtly changing direction. All the feathers lying together on the bird's body repeat this smooth contouring, and though a wing might be out-stretched, pointing in an opposite direction to the bird's tail, somehow the feathers sweep in an unbroken arc. It is these directional changes which can be captured by revising the traditional methods of working satin stitch and returning to *opus plumarium*. Where, according to the rules of satin stitch, the individual stitches lie side by side, in *opus plumarium* each stitch disappears beneath its predecessor, ultimately allowing the description of a complete 360° (see Fig 7).

The brimstone butterfly is also one of the earliest harbingers of spring, and as it bears one of the least complex of all wing patterns, it is also an excellent start-ing point from which to explore the treasure house represented by these most beautiful and diverse insects. Whilst the sweep of the wings may be conveyed in the same way as the arc of the primrose's petals, we first meet the problems here of a feature to be included within the *opus plumarium* – a spot on the wing. Almost every butterfly and moth is marked in some way with spots or zig-zagging which must be incorporated within the body of the embroidery, not superimposed on top. If it is worked over the top of the existing embroidery, it will look like a spot 'on top', whereas on the actual butterfly the transition between yellow wing and

. . . .

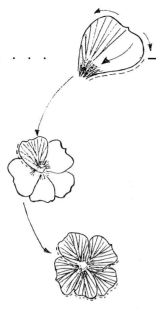

Fig 7 △

Each petal of the primrose should be treated separately. Initially, take a long single stitch down through the middle of the petal and then work outwards to the edge, completing one side before beginning the other. Radial lines shown suggest only about one in four of the stitches needed to complete each motif, in order to simplify the directional concept. Work one petal at a time, and the flower head will gradually be built up, eventually encompassing a full 360°

PLATE 12 >

The large tortoiseshell butterfly (Nymphalis polychloros) has suffered badly since the decimation of elm trees by Dutch elm disease. In England it is now restricted to small areas in East Anglia and Kent (although a few are occasionally recorded further afield). If you are determined to see one in the flesh they now rely upon willows, aspens and similar trees for food and shelter, but sadly a far more reliable source of reference must be textbooks.
The oxlip (Primula elatior) is now even rarer than its close cousin the cowslip, though once they were used by the armful to make a heady country wine 9 x 9cm (3¹/₂ x 3¹/₂in)

orange feature is completely smooth. A new technique must be employed. The spot must be worked first as a patch of *opus plumarium* in the correct direction, bearing in mind the sweep of the wing. Then the surrounding area must be worked around it. I have dubbed this the 'dalmatian-dog' technique, best summed up as follows; do not work a white dog and then put on his spots, work the spots first and then the dog around them!

Plate 12 shows all of these techniques used with greater precision, on slightly more complicated subjects. The central core of each of the oxlips has been used as the pivot point for the radial use of *opus plumarium*, and the complex pattern on the wings of the large tortoiseshell has been worked sequentially, beginning with the blue starring and followed by all the surrounding features. It is the type of study to save, perhaps, for a future spring, when a summer and autumn full of such challenges have been enjoyed.

BLACK MAGIC

The old country name for bindweed, one of the hedgerow's most common plants, was Devil's guts, which will no doubt ring a bell with many an enthusiastic gardener who has tried unsuccessfully to rid himself of the persistent, yet attractive

< *PLATE 13*

Along the sides of country lanes surrounding my home, hedge bindweed is common and in places the flowers become deeply tinged with pink. They attract various insects, which pollinate the flowers by using their long tongues to reach into the recesses of the trumpet-shaped flowers, which themselves present a challenge to the sketcher (see Fig 8).
The meadow cranesbill (Geranium pratense) also has its counterpart in the cottage garden, where it may be easier to spot than in an overcrowded hedgerow
10.25 x 21.75cm (4 x 8¹/₂in)

weed. The stems of the bindweed revolve anti-clockwise to surround and strangle anything they touch, and can complete a full circle in under two hours. The trumpet-shaped blooms of the hedge bindweed in particular are beautiful, staying open into the night, and remaining open through the night if there is a full moon (hence the Westcountry name of 'morning glory').

There are few plants which do not include stems in their structure, just as there are few embroidered studies which do not include stem stitch as an integral part of their format, and uninhibited by foliage the bindweed makes an excellent model through which to explore this expressive stitch (see Plate 13). Working on a black background allows us temporarily to ignore the 'shadowing effect' and concentrate upon the nature of the stitches themselves without the encumbrance of an additional line in close proximity. The practical application of stem stitch may be found in any embroidery textbook, but when using the stitch freely it needs to be long, thereby allowing a free sweep of stitches to describe a gentle curve and smaller ones when the curve becomes tighter. In Plate 13 the stems of the bindweed are sinuous and curve lazily. The stitches are long, and overlap only to about one-third of their length. Where the smaller buds of the cranesbill (beneath the larger plant) droop over, the same stitch is used much more tightly and the short, individual stitches overlap to at least half of their respective lengths.

◁ *Fig 8*
The coiling stem of the bindweed should be worked with bold stem stitching, changing direction as indicated

A coiling stem must be seen to be altering direction smoothly, and it is virtually impossible to work the stem stitch in the same way to describe a right curving line and a left curving line. It is important that the stitches should not 'fight' the curve. Where the top of the stitch is to the right of its predecessor, the curve will naturally form sweeping away to the left, and vice versa. To change direction a transitional stitch must be made. This is not a stem stitch but a split stitch, like the points at a railroad junction, giving the embroiderer breathing space before setting off again in a new direction.

◁ *PLATE 14*
'Convolvulus' was a name once applied not only to the bindweed (Convolvulus arvensis) *but also to its larger relative the hedge bindweed (see Plate 13). Artistically they present the same challenge and many of the same characteristics. The smaller bindweeds are more delicate and are better companions to smaller insects such as the peach-blossom moth* (Thyatira batis) – *so called because of its delicate colouring. The pink-within-white markings are excellent subjects on which to practise the dalmatian-dog technique, and the lower wings will allow relief in the shape of some simple* opus plumarium!
13 x 8cm (5 x 7in)

Fig 10 >

As a rule of thumb, the number of species in a hedge is a guide to its age; count a hundred years for every different species. Rose, hawthorn, broom, bramble, privet and holly would place this hedgerow's origins at the turn of the 1300s. A rough drawing like this in your sketchbook begins to build up a familiarity with different shrubs as they appear in the middle distance. Later, other details can be added

Fig 9 ▽

Motifs from the Maaseik textiles showing (right) coiling interlace of a trefoil plant, (upper left) a lizard and (lower left) a cat

These techniques were well known more than ten centuries ago when the Anglo-Saxons were creating embroideries which we now know were forerunners of *opus Anglicanum*, English work which was to become prized throughout the known world as the supreme example of embroidered art. In the fabulous convoluted designs of Anglo-Saxon gold and silk work, the outlines of the motifs were worked with stem and split stitch, following the curves and tortuous interlaces. Much of the inspiration sprang from the countryside, wild and untamed by man, where the spirits of tree and plant interwove with those of man and animal to create the 'Wyrd' or Web of Life. The bindweed had little medicinal value and was destructive, but the influence of its coiling interlace is easy to spot.

THE DARLING BUDS OF MAY

It is rare in nature to see a single flower or leaf silhouetted against nothingness. It is a liberty which we can sometimes take artistically (especially on black) for special effect, but for realism it is important to be able to superimpose features of a design on top of one another.

Stand beneath an apple tree during blossom time and look through the branches. You will see a jumble of blossom and young leaves tossing in the spring breeze, some full face towards you, some turning away, some ragged and some hardly out of bud (see Plate 15). There is constant movement and a complete

PLATE 16 ▽
This reconstruction of a principal strip from the Maaseik embroideries, which are believed to have been commissioned by King Offa of Mercia as an ambassadorial gift to the Court of Charlemagne at the turn of the ninth century, is shown life size 9cm (3¹/₂in) high. Many features of the medieval countryside are easily identifiable. In the first column, top left, is a deer or a wild horse, and below is a cat. In the second arcade from the right, two ducks are shown beneath a tree, whilst strange zoomorphic animals intertwine with foliage throughout the length of the piece. The strip continues in like manner for 63cm (24¹/₂in)

inconstancy of form. Here your sketchbook must come into play, not to create a finished masterpiece – for remember the only person who need ever see its contents is yourself – but simply to record the haphazard frivolity of those dancing blossoms. Make a haphazard sketch! If spring is wearing on and blossoms have already begun to fall, pick up a handful and drop them on the ground. Explore how they overlap, and enjoy the shimmering texture of the petals. Make a rough sketch of the way they lie. Later, if inspiration moves you to make a finished embroidery of the subject, they will not just be distant images, but real three-dimensional subjects.

You have taken your sketch home, perhaps many months later you have tidied it up. It is now transferred onto fabric ready to be brought to life. How to capture that bright, tossing cluster? The laws of perspective tell us that the features of a design which are nearest to us, and therefore uppermost, are to some extent going to catch our attention first. It is therefore wise to begin with these features and work the remaining motifs around them. It is also true that it is easier to build up a picture from a central point and work outwards than to begin at the extremities and leave 'holes' to be filled in later by the principal features. So, having once decided that the primary blossoms will be worked first, we must decide how to interpret them. The pollen mass in the centre of each flower is a dusty yellow, each anther supported by a slender filament which is invisible when the blossom is seen full faced but noticeable when seen from an angle. This central core must be worked first. Slender, straight stitches form the filaments, and the pollen is indicated by tiny seed stitches, randomly placed, so that each flower seems to have a tiny, fragile pom-pon at its core.

For the first time we must discuss the radial stitching of *opus plumarium* as it applies to flowers seen at an angle and not wholly facing the viewer. If we allow that for each flower, a full 360° must ultimately be described, it is easy to work our way around the open blossoms. But for those seen from the side, or only partly open, it must be borne in mind that the angle of the individual stitch, from the outside of the petal to the core of the motif, must still form a uniform part of that circle, whether we are looking at the back of the petal, its side, or indeed its reflex. It is a complicated concept, made only slightly simpler by a visual explanation (see Fig 11), but one which is central to the realistic interpretation of flowers. Suddenly it will fall into place.

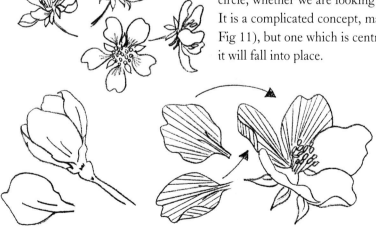

◁ *Fig 11*
When a petal is seen to curve, the underside comes into view. The shallow dish of the apple blossom must continue to sweep around the central part of the flower and the angle of the stitches must vary to accommodate its irregular shape

◁ *PLATE 15*
'Rough winds do shake the darling buds of
May . . .', wrote Shakespeare, and to capture
this glorious disorder flowers must appear to be
tossing in and around each other. The all-
important shadow line, however, is still
necessary to throw each separate blossom into
relief. Here the imaginary light source comes
from almost immediately overhead, creating a
shadow towards the base of each motif,
including the goldfinch
9 x 10.25cm (3¹/₂ x 4in)

Most hedgerow apple trees (crab apples) have domesticated fruit somewhere in their ancestry, and as there are over 3,000 named varieties of apple under cultivation the wild stock is equally diverse. Some crab-apple blossoms are white and virginal, others are tinged with pink or streaked with an even darker shade. Many of the finch family are very destructive to early blossoms, nipping them off in the bud, having initially been attracted by their brightness and then found them inedible. A 'charm' of goldfinches amongst the wild crab-apple blossom would be considered a great deal less charming in an orchard!

SNAKES AND LADDERS

The snake's head fritillary (Plate 17) is now found only rarely in the wild, but its sinuous form is an ideal subject through which to bring together the use of stem stitch and the technique of overlaying one feature upon another to create a natural interlace and give interest to a picture. The leaves of the snake's head are themselves

PLATE 17 ▷

*The name fritillary is given not only to the now
rare snake's head lily* (Fritillaria meleagris)
*but also to a family of spotted butterflies, whose
intricate wing patterns have much in common
with the chequer-board design of the flower.
Cultivated versions of the snake's head can
now be bought for the garden, although as
recently as the 1930s they were to be found in
great profusion in areas of England's
Westcountry, especially around the village of
Oaksey, near Cirencester in Gloucestershire,
(giving rise to the local name Oaksey Lily)*
9 x 18cm (3$^1/_2$ x 7in)

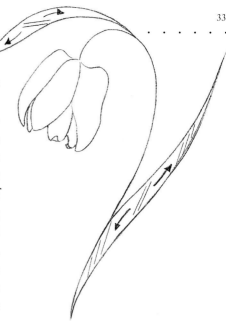

snake-like, fine and fragile. At their base, they wrap themselves around the stems of the plant, curving first inwards and then outwards towards their tip.

The stems are obvious candidates for the use of stem stitch and offer excellent scope for changes in the length of the stitch, to describe the varying steepness of their curves where the heads and buds of the flower droop over. However, the techniques required for the leaves almost fall between two stools, too slim for a satin stitch, too fat for a stem stitch. In truth the stitch needed must be a hybrid of both. Perhaps we should call it snake stitch. It takes the principle of not fighting the curve to the ultimate limit. Each leaf should be treated as a separate entity, but with two halves, one curving in direction 'a' the other in direction 'b' (see Fig 12). By beginning each leaf at its centre and working outwards, first towards the tip and then inward to the stem, the curve can be created smoothly, starting with those leaves and features in the foreground and then receding. The 'belly' of the leaf, if there is one, will then form naturally at the thickest point.

The chequer-board pattern on the flowers of the lily are one of the most extraordinary in the whole of nature and the technique, 'laddering', used to re-create it will be discussed later (see page 73).

As the last few weeks of spring give way to summer the vibrant colours of the bittersweet and warm, sun-drenched copper of the silver-washed fritillary (Plate 18) herald the coming of a new season.

Fig 12 △

Direction 'a' is always from the centre to the outermost tip of a sinuous leaf or other shape, direction 'b' from the centre to the base. Take an initial stitch in the centre of the leaf to establish the directional sweep and allow it to evolve naturally, becoming more oblique as the fine point at the apex of the leaf is reached

◁ *PLATE 18*

Bittersweet (Solanum dulcamara) *is a distant relative of the potato, but its purple and yellow flowers are as spectacular as those of its cousin are dull. They are a rare treat for the embroiderer of countryside subjects – a genuinely exotic show among the more predictable pinks and reds of high summer, and when these die they are followed by berries, at first green, then yellow and finally deep pillar-box red. As shown, the flowers may be worked very simply but to great effect. Here they are worked as a perfect foil for the silver-washed fritillary* (Argynnis paphia), *in which the elaborate zig-zagging and spotting take the dalmation dog technique almost to excess.*
9 x 9cm (3^1/2 x 3^1/2in)

HELEN
STEVENS

CHAPTER TWO

THE WOODLAND FLOOR

*The May month flaps its glad green leaves like wings
Delicate-filmed as new spun silk ...*

'Afterwards'
Thomas Hardy

◁ *PLATE 19*

The lesser periwinkle (Vinca minor) *has come into bloom and the quick-growing herb Robert* (Geranium robertianum) *has already matured from seed in a single season. The blossom of the horse chestnut* (Aesculus hippocastanum) *is among the most beautiful of all the large trees, with yellow, gold, pink and crimson centres appearing at the same time in a single tall candle of blossom.*
Young grey squirrels (Sciurus carolinensis) *leave the tree-top nest at about ten weeks old. The great spotted (or barred) woodpecker* (Dendrocopos major) *is most easily differentiated from the lesser spotted woodpecker by its size, but a juvenile may appear similar to its smaller cousin, especially as its red cap (which fades as it matures) is a shared characteristic. The distinctive shoulder bars in white, however, give the game away.*
Embroidery shown life size:
38 x 29.5cm (15 x 11¹/₂ in)

PLATE 20 (opposite)
The yellow archangel (Lamiastrum galeobdolon) *is a close relative of the white and red dead nettles but its bright-yellow flowers streaked with orange-red are more spectacular. The pretty pink wood anemone* (Anemone nemorosa) *has earned the country name of 'smell-fox', so pungent is its odour. In North America the Yorkshire fog grass* (Holcus lanatus) *is called velvet grass, whereas the English name is directly descended from the Old Norse 'fogg', which actually means grass. The small tortoiseshell* (Aglais urticae) *is one of Britain's commonest butterflies. The earliest specimens are those which have hibernated throughout the winter, appearing somewhat shabby and dull compared with the newer generations which begin to appear in June*
14 x 18cm (5¹/₂ x 7in)

· · · · · · · ·

THE WILD WOOD

'The Wild Wood' in Kenneth Grahame's *The Wind in the Willows* was a place of foreboding in winter. Even in the summer Ratty and his friends were wary of wandering too far into its recesses for fear they might become lost, prey to its dark places and even darker inhabitants. It is true that in spring, when we expect to find busy activity under the canopy of the oakwood, there seems often to be a curious stillness about its glades and paths and in the coppiced beechwood the sensation that something just around the corner is purposefully staying out of sight.

It is, of course, all an illusion. There is as much life and friendly natural interaction here between species as in the open sunny grasslands, but on the woodland floor the plants and insects go about their business of survival quietly. The myriad different greens and subtly changing textures of leaves and grasses are a cool satiny fabric on which flowers and early fruits are embroidered like tiny jewels; ruby-red wild strawberries and their pearl-white flowers, periwinkles of amethyst and sapphire forget-me-nots. Above this finery the insect life is all movement – butterflies dance, sometimes falling suddenly from the canopy overhead, and spiders weave their webs for the unwary.

Plate 20 is designed to capture this low-level activity as if seen from within,

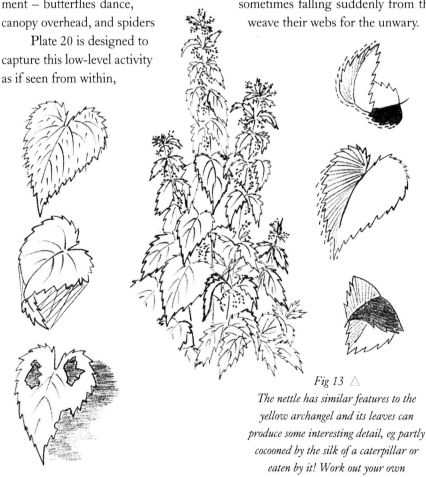

Fig 13 △
The nettle has similar features to the yellow archangel and its leaves can produce some interesting detail, eg partly cocooned by the silk of a caterpillar or eaten by it! Work out your own 'shorthand' to remind you of light and dark, sunshine and shade.

not above. Lying full length on the forest floor, sketchbook propped a few inches from one's nose may be an undignified way to achieve a preliminary sketch, but it is an immediate method of transportation into that 'other world' where the minutiae of nature takes on major proportions. As has been discussed previously, unless the embroiderer is a brilliant and spontaneous pencil artist any sketch made under such circumstances will be rudimentary and intended only as a guide, but in the flickering, dappled light of the wood certain points must be carefully noted. Even though the intention may be to work the piece on a black background (and many intricate woodland subjects seem to call for this as a foil to their complexity) the directional light source is still important, despite the fact that a 'shadow line' will not be called for. The yellow archangel has particularly dark glossy leaves above, whilst underneath they are pale and almost downy. As a light breeze gently rocks the plant from side to side these contrasting textures play both in light and shadow, and when the green silks are chosen for their working, it is important to be able to remember where each fell.

Wood anemones and wild strawberries may overlap in their flowering and fruiting times and their simple, open faces are ideal for novice sketcher and embroiderer alike. Not all grasses are green, and their simple blades are often overshadowed

PLATE 21 ▷

Wild strawberries (Fragaria vesca)*, the forerunners of the domestic strawberry, have an exquisite flavour. They multiply by shooting out long runners (ideal practice for stem stitch!) so eating the fruit does not threaten the survival of the plant.*

The comma butterfly (Polygonia c-album) *is another success story, and its population is on the increase. It is a frequent visitor to woodland glades where, like the tortoiseshell, it will obligingly bask for hours in warm sunshine. Butterflies' antennae immediately differentiate them from moths, which, with a few exceptions, do not have 'clubbed' antennae. When embroidering the antenna of a butterfly, the finest gauge thread must be used singly in a long straight stitch, tipped with a club of shorter stitches. Antennae are particularly effective when laid over some other feature of the picture, as shown here, to give a three-dimensional aspect 9 x 9.5cm (3¹/2 x 3³/4in)*

by their 'flowers', as the outer scales of the numerous spikelets are frequently pinkish or purple as in the case of this Yorkshire fog grass, common in open woodlands. Notice how the flower heads are arranged on grasses; they are often overlooked and their design potential is staggering. They are simple to draw and simple to interpret in groups of stocky seed stitches worked together and living up to their name by creating 'seeds'.

STRAWBERRIES AND CREAM

A closer acquaintance with the wild strawberry plant is an ideal method of introduction to still more frequently occurring shapes and subjects (see Plate 21). The simple regular flower with its prominent sepals is as easy to interpret as the primrose and apple blossom and offers scope for practising both sketching and embroidery from various angles. Stems and runners are clear candidates for stem stitch, and now for the first time we have a subject for the exploration of the ovate leaf form. Botanically speaking, the wild strawberry has three leaflets making up each leaf, but for ease of description we may treat each leaflet as an entity in its own right. It is slightly serrated (sharp toothed), bright green above and pale beneath. Once an initial sketch is tidied up and transferred to fabric, interpretation can begin, and these rules will hold true for virtually every centrally veined leaf of any species.

Working on a pale background allows use of the shadow line. With light falling almost directly from above the underside of each leaf (including the underside of each serration) should be shadowed (see page 10) and the upper angles left free. The central vein of each leaf is worked as a continuation of the stem. The veins carry the life-blood of the plant, and are to the leaves what the pollen mass at the centre of a flower appears to be, the core from which the 'liveliness' of the stitches must radiate. In simple, regular flowers, as we have seen, stitches must ultimately radiate 360° from their core. In centrally veined leaves, that core (the

Fig 14 △
Grasses can be sinuous and highly decorative. Explore the different ways they behave, and sketch in their whiskers. These will be too fine to transfer onto your fabric, so it is important that you have a record of them in your sketchbook

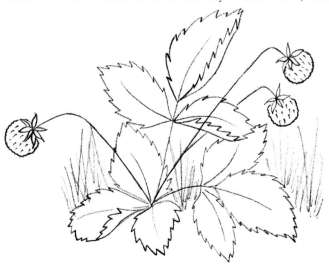

◁ *Fig 15*
A simple sketch of wild strawberries invites interpretation in embroidery

PLATE 22 ▷

The meadow cranesbill (Geranium pratense)
*is a member of the widespread geranium
family, related to the stork-bills, herb Robert
and the many garden geraniums. The veining
on the inside of the petals guides nectar-hungry
bees towards the pollen at the centre of the
flower, ensuring the reproduction of the plant.
The common name comes from the shape of the
attractive seed heads standing proud and
haughty as cranes and storks, which were
once common in England.*

*Bumble bees, in this case the white-tailed
variety* (Bombus lucorum) *are particularly
fond of the long-flowering meadow cranesbill –
their pollen sacks become heavy and
cumbersome after long periods enjoying the
flower's nectar. Aerodynamically speaking, the
bumble bee should be too heavy to fly –
capturing its lumbering in-flight activity will
be discussed later 9 x 9cm (3¹/₂ x 3¹/₂in)*

'growing point') is elongated into a line. Once again, the stitches would describe a complete circle, but they are constantly slipping downwards towards the base of the vein, smoothly, boldly, and with the use of a lighter shade on uppermost surfaces being enhanced by the way in which 'real' light, as opposed to the imaginary light source, will catch the stitching.

On the meadow cranesbill, the deeply lobed and toothed leaves, often comprising five or six leaflets form a rosette at times and ideally illustrate this circular progression, (see Plate 22). The outermost tip of each leaflet thrusts towards a different compass point. An imaginary circle, or oval, could be drawn joining the points, and from each of these the stitches slip smoothly towards the base of the leaf.

Returning to the strawberry, where leaves curl (reflex), the underside becomes visible. This is worked in a paler shade as closely matched to nature as possible and is worked at an identical, but opposite, angle to the upper surface of the leaf. If the leaf could be unfurled and opened out flat the angle of the stitches would remain the same. Descriptions of technique are always better accompanied by visual aids, so pick a few simply shaped leaves and examine the way in which the light plays upon their surfaces.

The fruit of the wild strawberry is a joy and it would be a rare artist who could resist the temptation of eating the model! The shape is simple and familiar,

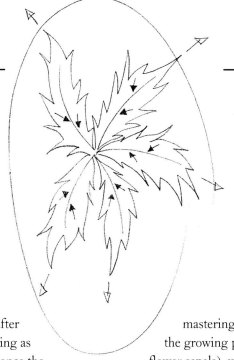

◁ *Fig 16*
Open arrows indicate the outward thrust of
each radial leaf, whilst the black arrows show
the direction in which the stitches should slip
down towards the core of the motif

and easy to interpret after   mastering the vagaries of
flowers and leaves. Using as   the growing point the rosette
at the top of the fruit (once the   flower sepals), work the stitches
up to meet it, shortening them as the perspective allows less sight of the curve
towards the edge of the motif. (Don't forget the shadow line beneath the fruit.)
For highlights introduce a few strands of slightly lighter thread on uppermost surfaces, and overlay tiny seeds with seed stitch.

      The buds of the meadow cranesbill may be depicted in the same manner,
their detailing consisting not of overlaid seeds, but of wispy orange-green tips
which make the motif a delight for the designer. When the flower of the cranesbill
opens this shape is echoed by the stigma and stamens at the core, and the softly
rounded tissue-like petals often flop over or curl inward, allowing the use of the
'opposite angle' stitching previously described for the strawberry leaves.

◁ *PLATE 23*
Detail. The opposite-angle principle is
particularly effective when used on large
leaves, such as horse chestnut. The five leaflets
of the compound palmate leaf are each at a
different angle to the viewer. The central leaf
faces us and may be worked simply, all of the
others tossed by a light breeze present more of
their undersides than of their upper surfaces. It
is therefore particularly important to remember
the directional flow of the stitches as they would
appear on the upper side in order to reverse this
and keep the perspective correct

HONEYSUCKLE ROSE

The shimmering, pink-faced dog rose is not all it seems – this apparently delicate flower is the product of a hardy root stock. It is a tenacious climber and its claws are sharp. Often found in hedgerows or in more open settings where it can become the wild tangle of a briar-patch, in a woodland setting it thrusts ever upward towards the light and at the edge of a path or glade can reach astonishing heights.

Such a large, open-faced flower (still essentially simple and regular) requires the use of radial *opus plumarium* worked in two strata (see Plates 24 and 25). Working on black, we can become used to the technique without the encumbrance of the shadow line. First, the core of the flower, the pollen mass at the centre of the motif, is worked. To add drama to the costume of this particular English rose there are scattered yellow and brown specks and a few seed stitches in gold metallic thread. Then the radial stitching is begun. Remembering that the epicentre of the flower is the point to which all stitches must appear to run (although apparently 'disappearing' under the pollen mass), the first (inner) strata is worked (Fig 18). The second (outer), strata is then worked in like manner, smoothly blending into the first row of stitches and, where necessary to advance the angle of stitch to a greater degree, disappearing under its neighbour (see page 23). Where the petals curl upwards the 'opposite angle' principle applies (see page 41).

Fig 17 ▽

The wild rose is a shrub of many parts, each of which require careful study. A slim, fairly immature plant like this can produce large, showy blooms

HELEN
STEVENS

<PLATE 24

*Why the most familiar of the wild English
roses should be called the 'dog' rose is open to
speculation. The ancient Greeks believed that
its medicinal properties cured the bite of mad
dogs, the Romans called the shrub by the same
name* (Rosa canina) *which was directly
translated into English. A more familiar
explanation, however, is that it blooms
throughout the 'dog-days' of summer: perfect,
hot, sunny days when the hum of the bees is
louder than the lazy chirping of tired, brood-
weary birds. The buff-tailed bumble bee*
(Bombus terrestris) *is active throughout
the hottest months of the year*
10.25 x 19cm (4 x 7^1/$_2$in)

HELEN
STEVENS

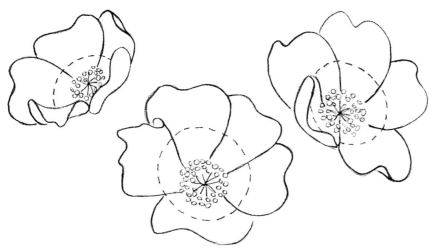

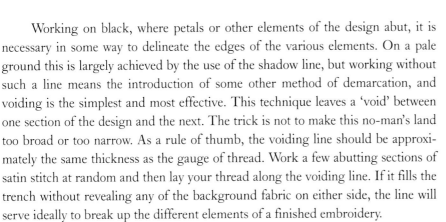

◁ *Fig 18*
The dotted line indicates where the first strata of radial stitching should end, to be followed by a second strata, blending smoothly into it. Where the line disappears under the curve of another petal (left and right), imagine that it continues smoothly, echoing the overall shape of the flower

Working on black, where petals or other elements of the design abut, it is necessary in some way to delineate the edges of the various elements. On a pale ground this is largely achieved by the use of the shadow line, but working without such a line means the introduction of some other method of demarcation, and voiding is the simplest and most effective. This technique leaves a 'void' between one section of the design and the next. The trick is not to make this no-man's land too broad or too narrow. As a rule of thumb, the voiding line should be approximately the same thickness as the gauge of thread. Work a few abutting sections of satin stitch at random and then lay your thread along the voiding line. If it fills the trench without revealing any of the background fabric on either side, the line will serve ideally to break up the different elements of a finished embroidery.

The leaves of the dog rose are ideal for the practice of the centrally veined leaf techniques described on pages 39–40. They are pinnate, symmetrically placed on either side of their stem, they curve freely and seem to arrange themselves instinctively into attractive poses.

The dog rose presents us with one more novelty – thorns. Like cat's claws they are hooked and sharp, tapering towards their point; and they appear asymmetrically along the length of the stem or branch. Worked in a series of overlapping straight stitches (four or five for a large prickle, only three or so on a small one) they must appear to join the stem smoothly and become an integral part of it.

Plates 24 and 25 illustrate perfectly the contrast between working on black and pale grounds. Where one allows for some slight artistic licence (see also Plate 20), the other calls for strict botanical detail. In neither case is the chosen background the main feature of the work. Indeed, the ultimate aim is to make that background 'disappear' entirely, as interest is focused on the subject matter. On black this is achieved by additional touches of drama. On a pale ground the very neutrality of the backdrop helps to create the desired effect. For this reason it is inadvisable to use white, which is too stark, too clinical and entirely alien in natural studies.

PLATE 25
(opposite)
A familiar butterfly of the hot summer months is the red admiral (Vanessa atalanta). It is a simple butterfly to sketch, as its markings are regular and uncomplicated, the bright-red bands creating a very satisfying contrast to the black outer wings when embroidery is underway. Two centuries ago it was called the 'Admirable' because of these characteristics, and pictured with the glowing pale pink of the wild rose, it captures the very essence of early summer 12.5 x 20.5cm (5 x 8in)

. . . .

Cream, pale oatmeal and other similar shades are ideal.

In an open, saucer-shaped flower such as the larger of the two blooms in Plate 25, the importance of the shadow line is well illustrated, but where the curl of the petal brings what would be its lower edge uppermost and into relief against the main body of the flower, the shadow line must follow the belly of the petal, shading the curve itself. Only in places does the shadow line serve to separate the planes, and here, as on the black background, voiding must be employed to break up the colour, which may be identical in both sections. The curl and curve of leaves follows the same principle.

Leaves in all their many forms are among the most beautiful and diverse of all nature's subjects, but the most strikingly formed can become dull and uninteresting if seen only as flat and two-dimensional. To be seen to best advantage their natural flexibility and liveliness must be captured, and to this end it is worth breaking off to gain some understanding of their structure and how they behave seen from different angles. The same principles hold true for a complex deeply toothed leaf as for a simple ovate form. The most important feature to 'get right' is the central vein. When drawing leaves, this midrib should be described with one continuous line, which must appear to be unbroken however much it may curve, and whether or not part of it is invisible. It must always flow smoothly and never appear fractured. Pick a simple curving leaf, such as one from a domestic rose bush, and hold it at eye level (see Fig 19). The unbroken line of the midrib will be obvious; draw it smoothly, and sketch in the outer edges of the leaves afterwards. Then look at it head-on and repeat the process. As soon as you understand the perspective of the leaf the terrors of freehand sketching will begin to disappear and your confidence will be boosted. Once the finished design is transferred onto fabric, the 'invisible' sections of the central vein will, of course, have been omitted. Your stem stitch describing the midrib will only appear where it is actually needed. The magic of a three-dimensional leaf will have been achieved.

In the orchestra of flowers, if the bindweed is trumpet and wild rose the cymbal, then the honeysuckle must surely be the saxophone. It is as far different as possible from the simple regular bloom of the rose. It has an irregular number of flowers on every head, each comprising a long tube-like body with a lobed upper lip and a sensuously drooping lower lip. The stamens extend well beyond the

◁ *Fig 19*
When curving or curling, the central vein of a leaf should still appear to be continuous, as indicated by the dotted line

◁ *PLATE 26*

There is no more romantic flower than the
honeysuckle (Lonicera periclymenum),
symbol of love, constancy and wedded bliss. It
has formed a popular stylised embroidery motif
for centuries. No less vaunted has been the
beauty of the purple emperor (Apatura iris),
the subject of myriad poems and named 'iris'
after the Greek messenger of the Gods who
spoke through the rainbow. As elusive to
capture as the rainbow's end is the colouring of
the purple emperor. The purple-blue sheen of its
wings alters with every slight movement, and
it appears dull and lifeless in photographs.

If you are fortunate enough to see a purple
emperor, (in England they are mainly confined
to the forests of the south coast) try to catch the
colour with children's crayons. Otherwise, the
best source material is from Victorian painted
plates (butterflies were a favourite subject and
faithfully reproduced.) They were also
frequent victims of the butterfly collector and
may be found pinned to many a museum card –
'captured' in silk is surely a much better idea
9.5 x 9cm (3³/4 x 3¹/2in)

mouth of the flower, to be tipped with pollen-covered anthers of yellow gold. In the wild, honeysuckle is often pinkish in colour, though it may tend towards orange or purple, and its inside is white or buttery yellow. Capturing its form must be considered something of a challenge. Sinuous is certainly the right word to describe the tubular form of the flowers, and so the snake stitch explored in the previous chapter once again comes to the rescue. The smooth gradation of stitches from the belly of the flower outward to its mouth then in towards the core must not fight the curve of the design. The light catching the embroidery will then enhance rather than detract from the overall effect. Seen full face, the open mouth of the flower is depicted by only a 'wedge' of radial stitching (in two strata). The stamens are then overlaid with long straight stitches, tipped with a seed stitch of the appropriate colour.

CHAPTER THREE

SUMMER MEADOWS

Crown'd from some single herb or tree ...
all the flowers and trees do close
To weave the garlands of Repose.

'Thoughts in a Garden'
A. Marvell

SUMMER HARMONIES

In summer, ripe fields of cereal crops lie like folds of sun-bleached linen and the baled straw lies in irregular ranks: slub in honey-gold silk. In the hedgerow and wood, unless a second brood is on the way, small birds can for the first time since the courting days of spring take time for song, and many flowers and shrubs come into colourful bloom. It is a period of riotous colour, of blues, reds, mauves (in nature there is no such concept as a clash of colours), and a time when embroiderers may well feel they wish to extend their palette of shades. Photography can be a great aid now. Go out into the meadows and snap great swathes of colour. In long dark winter months it is difficult to recall the bright shades of summer without some aide-memoire. The combination of a snatch of colour and a wisp of sketch will bring it all back.

The full blown combination of colour and form, and the heady intertwining of species, is what summer is all about. The rose and the honeysuckle (Plate 28) climb together, but already some of the honeysuckle flowers have given way to fruit. This is an embroiderer's dream as different berries on the same head ripen at their own rate, showing scarlet, green and gold in juxtaposition. The weight of the berries pulls the stem down, creating curves.

◁ *PLATE 27*
The tiny harvest mouse (Micromys minutus) *is Europe's smallest mouse, so light that it hardly even bends the stalks of the cereals in which it makes its nest.*
The corn marigold (Chrysanthemum segetum) *is a close relative of the more common ox-eye daisy, and thrives on newly or once cultivated ground including the headlands of conservation-conscious farms. Its deep golden butter-coloured petals contrast pleasingly with the delicate blue of the pale flax* (Linum bienne). *Wild flax prefers a slightly damp location, in common with the pink ragged robin* (Lychnis flos-cuculi).
In this study a distant landscape has been framed by the foreground features. The colours used to create the distant scene are also used in the foreground features as a link.
Embroidery shown life size:
38 x 28cm (15 x 11in)

PLATE 28 (opposite)
One reason for the success of the chaffinch (Fringilla coelebs) *is its ability to feed on a wide variety of food, which means that it is to be found in diverse settings. Nobody should be at a loss to find a breeding pair to study. When feeding young, the chaffinch's diet is broadly based upon insects, though at other times of the year its typical seed-eater's beak means that it is well equipped to deal with beechmast, grain and other hard seeds. In colour the chaffinch is not dissimilar to the peacock butterfly and the two together in any picture create a delightful harmony. In this study, both colour and shape are designed to lead the eye from feature to feature, finally encompassing the whole*
23 x 33cm (9 x 13in)

▽ *Fig 20*
A relatively simple (but rare) flower such as the corn cockle can be sketched from life as a single study and later put into a more complicated setting, such as Plate 34

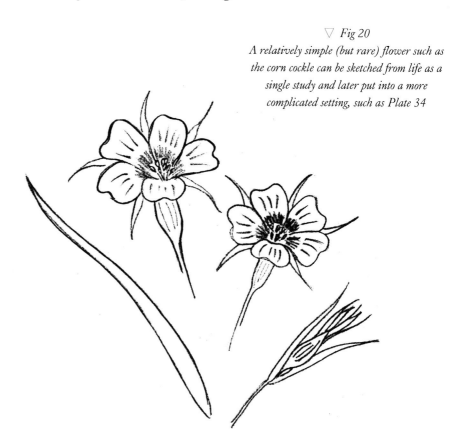

Beneath its two more lofty companions the bramble is still in flower, not ready yet to offer up its autumn blackberries. The blackberry belongs to the same family order as the rose and the wild strawberry and their leaves are not dissimilar. The principles for realistic interpretation discussed earlier also apply here. Plate 29, a detail of the larger study, illustrates this and brings us, for the first time, into close examination of birdlife.

The chaffinch is not known for its timidity, and as there may be as many as almost fifteen million dispersed throughout the whole of the British Isles (and many million more beyond) it is an excellent bird to observe. Its shape is pleasantly elliptical. The body and head in rough outline are a series of decreasing ovals. Its colour and markings are well delineated and ideal for the study of feathers and plumage.

As has been discussed, the principle of *opus plumarium* is to allow a smooth flow of stitching without interruption. First, certain features of the bird must be worked as reference points and centres of attention. Obviously, beak and eye head

Fig 21 △

The chaffinch has well defined markings and a compact shape, making it the perfect bird on which to become familiar with the blending technique between fields of colour. Long wing and tail feathers should be treated individually. As it stands, this design is stark. The bird should be set into surroundings of foliage or grasses to give it a sense of reality

PLATE 29 ▷

The centre of attention for this chaffinch is, of course, the spider's web and its edible contents! Spiders' webs provide an intriguing and attractive device within a hedgerow setting.

this list, and as ever, the shadow line gives the bird a 'place' within the imagined light source of the overall picture. Where the dividing line between certain colour markings is sharp, allow stitching to terminate in a fairly straight line, and begin the next strata of stitching similarly (without voiding, as you are working in a continuous plane) such as on the collar of the chaffinch. Where colours merge gently, such as on the underbelly, allow them to mix gradually, lightening the overall effect with the addition of single strands of thread. Always begin at the bird's head (treat the beak as the 'growing point' similar to the core of a flower) and work backwards towards the tip of the tail. Having established the principle of strata progressing backward, remember that each individual stitch should be taken inward, so that it will merge smoothly with its precursor. (See Figs 22 & 23 and the explanation of strata stitching of flowers in Fig 18).

The naturalistic interpretation of a bird's wings can be among the most challenging of projects for the embroiderer. Whether in repose (Plate 29) or in flight (Plate 30) they present a whole new range of textures and directional considerations.

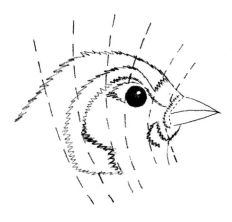

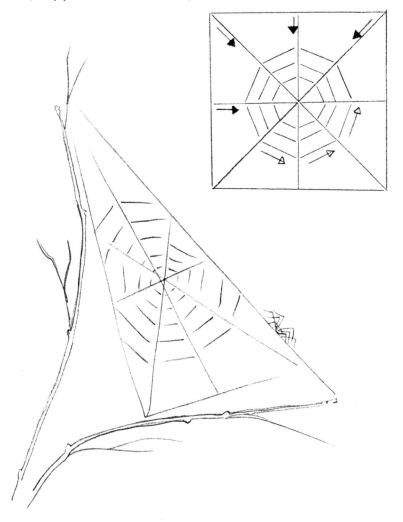

△ Figs 22 and 23 △

Fig 22 shows the directional stitching on the chaffinch's head. (The eye should be worked in a series of perpendicular stitches to contrast as much as possible with the lie of the feathers.) Fig 23 shows the cut-off point for each strata of stitching. Roughly speaking the radial sweeps coincide with the different colours and markings on the heads. The dotted line to the extreme right delineates the tiny band of feathers at the base of the beak. The next dotted line terminates the band of stitching describing the black head markings. The third and fourth lines outline the eye and eye stripe, and so on

◁ Fig 24

The spider's web can be as regular or random as the artist chooses. In every case the spokes are worked first. The diagram (above right) shows an eight-spoke web. The spokes are formed by four directional stitches as shown by the black arrows. Then the circular filaments are added by whipping the spokes, that is by taking a tiny stitch around and behind each one and stretching the thread between them

When closed, each rank of feathers lies over the other in a series of planes which must be delineated either with shadow lines or voiding, but in flight each of the long primary feathers is revealed to a greater extent and must be treated accordingly. Again, close inspection of feathers found on country walks will be of great help. From the central vein of each feather (its quill), the filaments radiate at an angle outward towards the edge and tip. This must be captured by stitching, in exactly the same way as the shape of a leaf is described by the outward sweep of the stitches. Working from the tip of the feather towards its base, the upper side should be completed first. If there is a gradation in colour this should be achieved gradually as the feathers taper. Tail feathers can be treated in the same way, but at all times remember that the overall sweep must be harmonious. There must be no sharp change in direction unless the planes are separated by a shadow line, or voiding.

FAMILY LIKENESSES

In becoming familiar with the face and form of one member of a plant family (as has been seen with the *Rosaceae*) it is often possible to move on to other families without learning their characteristics from scratch. The rosebay willowherb (Plate 30) is a lofty and elegant plant with plump top buds, and delicate flowers. The closed seed pods form a graceful arc and then burst open, scattering winged seeds

◁ *PLATE 30*

It is always pleasant to learn that an attractive wildflower is now actually more common than it was in the last century, and this is the case with the rosebay willowherb (Epilobium angustifolium)*. During the Victorian era it was transplanted into gardens as a rarity, and by the time of World War II it was so well established that it had once more escaped into the wild and even colonised the blitzed bomb sites of London's East End. Once established, as well as sending out great clouds of downy seeds to reproduce itself, it also produces a thick, woody root system which sends up new shoots at intervals along its length. Vetches* (Vicia sepium) *are among the earliest of all cultivated plants; (traces have been found in Iron Age settlements) and the broad bean, for instance, is a member of the vetch family. Their attractive appearance has helped to ensure their success.*

The blue tit (Parus caeruleus) *is another garden bird which is easy to observe and study. Its familiar colouring is much more subtle than it first appears – its bluish back is actually a mixture of many shades of green and blue, quite different from its bright-blue cap. Its underparts are yellow and grey. At the end of the breeding season the blue tit, exhausted by the rearing of up to thirteen fledgelings becomes quite dull in comparison with its early spring finery. If you find it difficult to find the correct, subtle shades of blue and yellow for resident English tits, European migrants which quite often arrive suddenly and in large numbers are much more brightly and brashly coloured*
20.5 x 35.5cm (8 x 14in)

◁ *Fig 25*
The best way to become completely familiar with a plant is to sketch it. The differences between the rosebay willowherb (left) and the great willowherb (right) become immediately apparent when compared side by side

like feathery snow flakes. It thrives on waste ground (its alternative name is the fireweed). There are four petals to each flower (though these appear doubled by the presence of four long purplish sepals) and many golden-tipped stamens.

Although it appears a complicated flower, the rosebay willowherb is made as simple to embroider as any 'regular' bloom by holding firm to the principles of radial stitching on both petals and sepals. The lower part of the plant has many different features so some thought must be given to which of those features should be worked first and which are secondary. As ever, perspective comes to the rescue. An easy rule to learn is that foreground features should be the first described, and those to the back of them worked subsequently. Therefore, in Plate 30, where the seed pods are directly between the eye of the viewer and the leaves, it is the pods which demand the initial attention, then the leaves. The leaves are simple, centrally veined affairs, which no doubt now present no problems at all, their directional stitching uninterrupted by the fact that they disappear in places 'behind' other features!

Beside its more elaborate cousin, the great willowherb (Plate 31) seems simple to capture in close-up, even more so on a black ground where voiding replaces shadow lines. Its four notched petals do not share their space with large sepals, but the delicate anthers are a feature, though paler than on the rosebay. The long, weeping-willow-shaped leaves are very similar.

PLATE 31 ▷

The great willowherb (Epilobium hirsutum) *thrives by the side of streams or even damp ditches and grows in dense banks of colour near my home where the caterpillars of the impressive elephant hawkmoth* (Deilephila elpenor) *make little impression upon its vigorous growth. The green and pink markings of the moth are among the prettiest sights to be seen in the evening sunlight, and, unlike butterflies whose markings are often sharp, and well delineated, the moth's markings merge softly one into the next — making them an ideal subject for the finest* opus plumarium. *The stocky body form is also quite different from that of the butterfly, and the antennae (not clubbed) are easily re-created by two slanting straight stitches in a fairly thick silver thread*
7.5 x 9cm (3 x 3¹/₂in)

◁ *PLATE 32*
Members of the mallow family have lived side
by side with man since earliest times and have
a particular link with textiles. When the leaves
are crushed and rubbed between the palms
with water, they produce soapy suds which
leave spun yarn soft and conditioned. The
common mallow (Malva sylvestris) *was*
used by the Romans as a cure for hangovers,
and in medieval times as an anti-aphrodisiac.
The flowers produce copious amounts of pollen,
picked up by bees as they move from bloom to
bloom, their pollen sacs full to the point of
overflow. The leaves of the common mallow
are broadly palmate, with (usually) five
principal veins. Treat each 'section' of the
leaf individually, following the same rules as
for centrally veined single leaves,
remembering that the lower side of each section
should be the darker, and building up the
whole leaf gradually
10.25 x 18.5cm (4 x 7¹/4in)

. . . .

PLATE 33 ▷

The pale clouded yellow (Colias hyale) *is
another butterfly best studied second hand, as it
is by no means common. Its darker cousin the
clouded yellow, is much more widespread and
may be found feeding on vetches and other
related plants. Similarly, the musk mallow*
(Malva moschata) *is somewhat less readily
found than the common mallow, but is worth
seeking out along roadsides and bridleways, as
its delicate shell-pink flowers produce an even
more striking contrast to the deeper purple
veining shared by both plants. The styles and
anthers protrude from the throat of the flower
and can be embroidered by a mass of tiny seed
stitches, cone shaped, firstly overlaying the
petal, then disappearing into a voided central
core* 10.25 x 10.5cm (4 x 3³/₄in)

Fig 26 ∧

*The simplified plan of a common mallow shows
the inward directional radial stitches indicated
by the black arrows, and the overlaid shooting
stitches by the open arrows*

· · · · · · · ·

Another family of flowers which shares many characteristics is the mallow (Plates 32 and 33). Its domestic relations can be found cultivated for profit (the cotton plant) and for pleasure (the stately hollyhock) and there are a number of variants which grow wild. The common mallow can grow up to 90cm (3ft) high, and its spectacular rich-pink flowers burst open like fireworks along the length of its strongly leaved stems. They are shot through with purple veins, turning the whole flower into a shimmering mixture of heliotrope and mauve. The best way to capture this effect is with a 'shooting' stitch. Having worked the main body of the flower the needle should be threaded with the deeper shade which is then super-imposed over the existing stitching. Work the stitches in opposition to the natural flow of those already worked. The radial stitching of the petals will have been effected from the outer edge inward so the overlaid stitches should be worked outward from the core.

The common mallow's close relative, the musk mallow, is a slightly more delicate version of its cousin. Though a paler pink, it shares the rich veining of the larger plant, though its leaves are much more deeply divided as they reach higher up the plant. Its lower leaves are kidney shaped and more like the five-pointed star-like leaves of the common mallow.

Mallows are well patronised by insects, and their long blooming period means that they are often good plants for observing butterflies. The pale clouded yellow butterfly occasionally arrives in Britain as early as May, though it is becoming increasingly rare, and is more likely to be seen in August or September. Its delicate yellow and grey markings, and well delineated spots are excellent subjects for the dalmatian-dog technique (see pages 23–4) and the darker markings on the wings near to the body of the insect may be effected by shooting stitches similar to those on the mallow petals. Butterflies on a black background use entirely the same principles as on a pale ground, with the exception that their antennae would not stand out effectively if shown in black themselves. One alternative is to use a touch of very fine gold thread.

CREATING AN IMPRESSION

Before turning to the broader canvas of landscapes (Plate 34), it is worth discussing close-up studies and distant scenes of the countryside. So far, we have examined the minutiae of nature and tried faithfully to capture its every detail, and whilst these criteria will still hold true (for what is distance without a foreground to throw it into relief?), a new dimension must be added. Look out of the window. Go for a walk. Focus on the middle distance and far horizon. You will be surprised at the number of features which you can identify without being able to pick out specific details. This is the basis of Impressionism. However, where the great masters of Impressionist painting, such as Monet and Manet, were able to capture a

Fig 27 ⋁
To begin an understanding of perspective, it is often useful to have a scene split up into a distinct foreground and background. Having worked the gateway in detail, one could now elaborate on the distant view and the foreground features

PLATE 34 ▷

A late summer's afternoon. By contrasting a distant landscape with a very detailed close-up in the same picture viewers are drawn into the piece, as if they are there among the tall sunlit grasses. The body of the bumble bee is formed by two almost spherical pom-pons, joined by a furry midriff. Each should be worked separately, with attention to the markings of the particular species. The wings, which in flight are just a whirring blur can be suggested by a series of graduated straight stitches in the finest gauge available, legs and antennae in a slightly thicker silk. Working on black, as in Plate 32, the wings must take their cue from the background fabric and be worked in a contrasting shade, and similarly the legs and antennae need greater emphasis. Where pollen sacs are in evidence, they may be either bright or dull yellow, or orange, according to the flowers which have been visited
Embroidery shown life size:
35.5 x 22cm (14 x 8¹/₂in)

distant subject with one touch of the brush, one flick of the palette knife, the embroiderer is destined to harder labour.

Plate 35 is a detail of the landscape shown in Plate 2. A wildflower meadow stretches away towards a distant hedge. In the foreground, daisies, knotweed, and long grasses frame the picture and these flowers recede with the scene, becoming more and more distant. Fewer and fewer individual details of each flower can be seen but even on the far side of the meadow each species can be identified. During the gradual recession only a small feature has been omitted at each stage. A detailed, shadowed study of a daisy has become a sketchy one, petals loosely centred on its pollen mass. The yellow core has then disappeared to leave only a corolla, which has in turn given way to a loose collection of white stitches in the rough shape of a distant flower. Similarly, a buttercup, which in close up would be portrayed as seen in Plate 36, becomes a loose gathering of petals and finally an impressionistic dab of colour among the grass. The grass itself is an important feature. In this particular study it needs to appear to surround the flowers, only allowing their heads to break its surface. To create this impression stitches are worked in the perpendicular: serried ranks of upstanding straight stitches, short in the far distance, becoming longer towards the foreground.

Trees, hedges, shrubs and distant fields all present their own challenges which will be explored as we stroll deeper and deeper into the embroiderer's countryside.

PLATE 35 >
The spider's web device works equally well superimposed over background feature, and, as it must be worked freehand, it can be incorporated anywhere in a picture as a finishing touch Actual size of detail shown: 10.25 x 8.25cm (4 x 3¹/₄in)

◁ *PLATE 36*
The bulbous buttercup (Ranunculus
bulbosus) *which can be suggested by a few
strategic stitches in a landscape (see Plate 35)
is a striking flower when portrayed
realistically, and in any wildflower meadow it
is a popular attraction for visiting butterflies.
The common blue butterfly is extraordinary in
that its wings contain no blue pigment! Its
bright colouring is produced by thousands of
iridescent scales which absorb all colours of the
spectrum except blue, making the wings glitter
exquisitely in sunlight*
7 x 9.5cm (2³/4 x 3³/4in)

Fig 28 △
*Poppy petals have the texture of fine tissue
paper; they flop and fall easily. It is advisable
to become familiar with the individual petals
before putting them together as a whole flower.
The directional stitches indicated on the petals
represent about one in six of the actual stitches
required in a fine gauge thread*

. . . .

POPPY DAYS

Poppies form one of the major foreground features in Plate 34. In most people's minds pillar-box-red poppies against the green and gold of ripening fields is an enduring image of summer. Still the bane of many farmers' lives, the poppy is a great survivor and in these more conservation-conscious times, with headlands left at the edges of many fields and herbicidal spraying less universal, they are once again creating great swathes of colour, interspersed with white patches of daisies and outcrops of yellow ragwort. Pick a poppy and before you get it home it will have died, the tissue paper petals limp as scraps of wet rag, its thin stem lifeless and floppy. Poppies must be sketched from life (or from good textbooks) and are a satisfying flower to master. The poppy has four petals, two smaller than the others, and the seed capsule at the centre of each flower is surrounded by black-pollened anthers. At the base of each petal there is often a blotch of black pigment enhancing the dramatic juxtapositioning of red and black (Fig 28).

The poppy design must be approached with caution. It looks simple and the temptation is to plunge in regardless, work the centre and then simply infill the petals with radial stitching. But beware. Think back to the poppies in situ, where

Simple designs can often be the most dramatic.
With only half a dozen or so colours,
this miniature study packs in all the vibrant
drama of the summer countryside
7 x 10.25cm (2³/₄ x 4in)

you could almost see right through the translucent petals. Whatever the gauge of thread you have been using for the rest of the design, work the petals in about half the width of thread. For once, do not be afraid to leave an occasional glimpse of the background fabric showing through the stitching. This holds true for studies on pale or black backgrounds (Plates 37 and 38). The stem of the poppy is flimsy and slight, and can be approached in various ways. In fairly close studies, use a single thread in one long strand (Plate 34). Alternatively, a gold metallic thread can be couched loosely but firmly to give a wavy, but completely smooth stem (particularly effective on black). For a very close study, such as Plate 38, the latter becomes unrealistic and a fine, even, graduated stem stitch must do the job. The leaves of the poppy, though deeply toothed, are essentially simple, centrally veined affairs which can also be enlivened by the addition of a little gold thread if desired. Once again, the gold thread is couched, preferably after the rest of the leaf has been worked.

◁ *PLATE 37*
The common poppy (Papaver rhoeas), *now a*
symbol of Remembrance Day, was associated
with fertility from Roman times and was
particularly admired as a motif by the Art
Nouveau movement. Its languid shape and
lissom appearance have an almost sensual
appeal from any angle. Poppies are particularly
useful in a study which is otherwise short of
vibrant colours; they allow the artist to
concentrate on details in neutral shades without
any fear that the overall picture will lack punch
15.5 x 16.5cm (6 x 6¹/₂in)

· · · · · · ·

CHAPTER FOUR

THE RIVER BANK

...There the chestnuts summer through
Beside the river make for you
A tunnel of green gloom, and sleep
Deeply above; and green and deep
The stream mysterious glides beneath

'The Old Vicarage, Grantchester'
Rupert Brooke

REFLECTIONS

< PLATE 39

To capture a feeling of distance, each feature of this design is portrayed from an unusual angle, which results in a picture full of activity and surprise.

The first leaves of the white willow (Salix alba) *to turn colour begin to fall quite early in the season. The grey wagtail* (Motacilla cinerea) *is an efficient aerial hunter, snapping up midges, mosquitoes, small dragonflies and mayflies on the wing. The emperor dragonfly is seen (bottom left) from the perspective of the water, as the insect darts forward towards its prey (see Plate 42). The giant lacewing* (Osmylus fulvicephalus) *is a sluggish flyer, preferring to emerge from its waterside retreat only in the evening when predators are fewer.*

Embroidery shown life size:
39.5 x 30.5cm (15¹/₂ x 12in)

PLATE 40 (opposite)
The kingfisher (Alcedo atthis) *is surely one of the most beautiful birds, and many legends exist to explain its beauty. One of the best relates to Noah, who, impatient for the return of the dove, sent out a kingfisher, then drab and grey with a long beak, to search for it. The kingfisher flew deep into the storm-clouds in its search and was struck by lightning, which left a strip of electric blue along its body. Then, rising above the clouds, the kingfisher flew too close to the sun and scorched its chest. When the poor bird finally got back to earth, the flood had subsided and the Ark was dismantled. To this day the kingfisher searches rivers and streams looking for it* 16.5 x 28cm (6¹/₂ x 11in)

Like a tattered chiffon veil, the reflection of sunlight on water flickers over the river bank. Everything is dappled, lazy, slightly mysterious. Water is the source of all life, and whether it is a tumbling highland stream, a majestic river, the marsh-covered edge of a water meadow, or a cool, secluded pool, it invites us to pause, slow down and add our reflections to its own.

From a distance it is often easy to spot the course of a river in a country landscape, as trees cluster about its banks and follow its meanderings. Whilst the elder statesmen, the oaks and chestnuts among them, occasionally like to get their feet wet, it is more likely that the river's edge will be crowded with younger and more lissom trees: willows, poplars, alders and aspen, many of which have leaves which shiver silver in the breeze as it reveals their delicately coloured undersides. All is movement, all is light and shadow and life.

Every species of tree is, of course, as different from the next as is each man from his neighbour, but the characteristics of most deciduous trees may be captured through embroidery with a broadly similar philosophy. The overall shape of a tree is dependent upon the structure of its trunk, branches and twigs beneath the foliage, so each individual must be first worked bare of foliage, and then dressed with the appropriate stitching, time consuming though this may be. Look at the structure of trees in the winter when their skeletal forms are etched sharply against the sky, or with a good countryman's handbook resist the temptation to look at the leafy summer illustrations and concentrate upon the structure of the winter tree. Sketch and then embroider the bare bones (simple, straight stitching is the best technique) and only then begin to apply the leaves. In summer, however well leafed

Fig 29 △
Before attempting to clothe the familiar oak tree with foliage, it is important to understand its winter structure

Fig 30 >
Trees along the bank are often lissom and
fragile in appearance, especially when bare of
foliage. Shown here are (left to right): aspen,
Lombardy poplar and white willow

a tree may appear there are always many gaps in the foliage through which the sky, or background landscape, can be seen. Allow these to form naturally as the leaves 'grow' on each branch and twig in the shape of tiny seed stitches. You may need over a thousand stitches to create a small tree, but the effect will be stunning.

HALCYON DAYS

The kingfisher is also known as the halcyon bird, symbol of calm water and days of peace and plenty. Certainly a quiet day on the river is made perfect by the sudden flash of colour and abrupt 'plop' as a kingfisher dives for its prey. Though usually most at home in slow flowing rivers, the kingfisher is also happy in the environment of flooded gravel pits and similar sites and will visit the coast, particularly in winter. Kingfishers need clean water, so to catch a glimpse you must choose your site carefully. They are so quick moving that sketching and photography are very difficult. (I once spent an idyllic week with friends cruising the Canal du Midi in southern France, surrounded by kingfishers but totally frustrated in my attempts at photography.) A good birdwatchers' handbook is probably the best means of becoming familiar with the bird, but beware when you create your embroidery design as the kingfisher is so much smaller than you might expect. Its body size is not much bigger than the average sparrow though it is much stockier. In Plate 40 scale has not provided a problem as the bird is in flight, ready to dive, and the small reed motif is purely decorative. In the cover illustration (shown also in Plate 40a) the yellow flag iris has to be designed to be in scale with the kingfisher.

In flight, its wings outstretched, the kingfisher is revealed at its most spectacular. The blue tit in flight design introduced the upper surface of an open wing; here the underside is on view. The large primary feathers and then the inner row

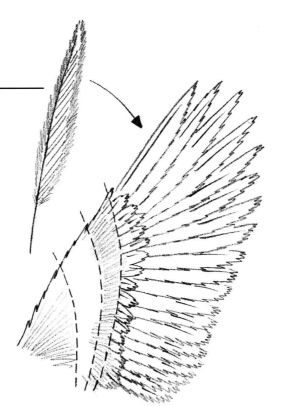

◁ *Fig 31*
Feathering of the inner wing is achieved by the use of radial opus plumarium. *The extent of each strata is indicated by the dotted lines. Primary and secondary feathers should each be treated individually*

of smaller feathers must each be worked separately, treating each individually as the filaments radiate from the central 'vein'. Then the main structure of the wing is worked outwards in radiating strata of *opus plumarium* from the bird's body, finally overlapping the base of the first row of feathers (see Fig 31). The upper surface of the more distant wing can be worked similarly. The main sweep of stitches on the bird's head, chest and lower body is directional.

Using the kingfisher as a model, we can develop the technique of voiding. So far, it has been used to differentiate between one plane and the next, as in the line created between the top of the bird's head and its wing (Plate 40). However, where certain parts of the body join, a hard, uniform line of voiding would be inappropriate. Here 'subdued voiding' comes into its own. This is well illustrated on the lower part of the kingfisher's body: just below its right foot where the belly joins the under-tail coverts, and lower down where the coverts give way to the longer tail feathers. Initially, work the voiding line in the usual way. Then, using a fine strand of thread, work straight stitches downward to break up the harshness of the line, leaving only an impression of the demarcation zone beneath. Subdued voiding can be a particularly useful technique when working an animal's fur, as will be discussed at length later.

Another very effective technique for small delicate features of plumage is 'ticking'. The electric-blue feathers on the kingfisher's head are not uniform in colour, even allowing for the gradual lightening from beak to neck. They are interspersed with bands of pale silver blue. Having worked the backward sloping, radial *opus plumarium* over the top of the head, tiny straight stitches may be worked over the top of the existing embroidery to create the desired effect. Always take the stitch in a backward direction, and make sure that it lies at exactly the same angle as the underlying work. If it crosses the directional flow it will look hard and unnatural; lying with the stitches it creates subtle highlights.

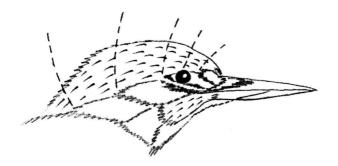

A third and final specialised technique used in Plate 40 is 'laddering'. We have mentioned this technique briefly before, in Plate 17, where it is used to convey the chequer-board pattern of the snake's head fritillary. Here it is used to create the scales of the fish, but it can also be employed to re-create any surface where small areas of anti-directional stitching would be effective. Work a strata of *opus plumarium*, gently sweeping in one direction. With your needle threaded identically, then weave backwards and forwards through the existing stitches (without going through the background fabric again) to make a complete new line which will lie loosely in the first strata and can be pushed into the correct position. Go through to the back of the work, come out at a point just below the first 'weave', and repeat the process, picking up alternative threads of the first strata. Repeat the process until the area to be covered is completed.

In the cover illustration (see Plate 40a) the irises have been worked in close detail, with extensive use of voiding and shooting stitches. They are worked densely in order that little of the black background fabric will show through the stitching, and the long grasses are created primarily by bold straight stitches, close together.

Both of these devices have been used more delicately in Plate 41. The lapwing belongs to the wader family so, though it favours arable ground of various kinds for its breeding and feeding, it is fond of areas which flood and become slightly marshy. The iridescent quality of its plumage appears from a distance to be wholly black and white, but on close inspection it is revealed to be green and even purple. The various types of feathering, smooth underneath and more rugged above, allow the practice of various types of infill stitching.

The slightly 'knock-kneed' appearance of the lapwing is a trait which it shares with other members of the wader family. Birds' legs are as individual as their plumage. The differences between, for instance, the fragile, stick-like legs of the robin and the long-toed, slightly stocky (for the size of its body) legs of the wren make them easily identifiable. Young birds' legs are often smoother than those of an older bird of a year or so's maturity, but the characteristic rings along their length still give them texture and break up what would otherwise be a smooth working of fairly solid stem stitch. Remember the shadow line to give reality, and work claws in the same technique as the rose thorns (described on page 45).

Remember to check the colour of the legs. On larger birds such as the lapwing and kingfisher it is an important part of creating a realistic whole.

DRAGONFLIES, DARTERS AND DAMSELS

Amid the sounds of the river bank, the flowing of the water, the tossing of leaves and the occasional splash as a fish rises or a bird dives, there can often be another sound to stir the curiosity. Its almost mechanical whir, metallic-blue body and shining wings make the dragonfly like some elegant prototype jet testing out its performance. Dragonflies are split into two primary groups: hawkers and darters. Darters, despite their name are the less agile, and spend long periods clinging to plants, making occasional sallies to attack prey or attract a partner. Hawkers, on the other hand, represent the Battle of Britain pilots and Bomber Command of the insect world rolled into one. The Emperor dragonfly is surely the most glamorous and spectacular insect imaginable.

Dragonflies present no problems for the sketcher, as they are symmetrical. Once the long, pencil-like body has been sketched, make the outline of one wing, and then reverse it to give an exactly matching pair. The largest of the insects in Plate 42 is an Emperor. Its thorax and abdomen are simply worked in straight stitching and the eyes are given their multi-lens appearance by mixing a strand of fine gold metallic thread with the silk thread in the needle.

The wings need more careful interpretation. Using the finest thread in your collection, work the outline of the wing followed by a series of fine radial stitches. These must then be caught down, alternately, by small stitches at right angles, building up the pattern like courses of brickwork. Miraculously, a honeycomb

◁ PLATE 41
The feathers of the lapwing (Vanellus vanellus) were once extensively used in the millinery trade, and the Victorian craze for feather embroidery also brought a number of the birds to grief, but thankfully the lapwing is still widespread. With permission from the landowner, take up a position in the open in an arable field on a winter's day. If you remain fairly still, the lapwings will soon carry on their usual routine of walking and feeding and you will be able to see at close quarters the effect of the winter sunlight on the bird's glossy plumage. The lapwing is a welcome visitor to farmland as it eats wireworms and other arable pests 16.5 x 14cm (6$\frac{1}{2}$ x 5$\frac{1}{2}$in)

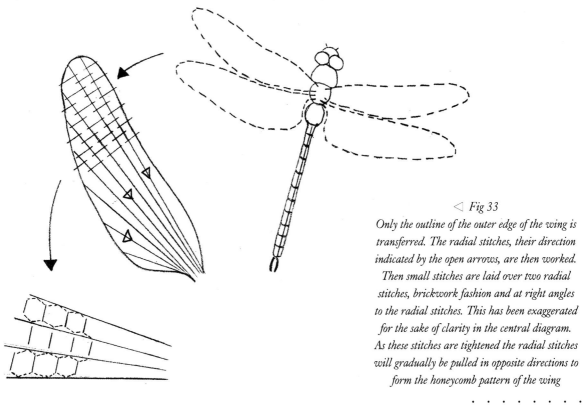

◁ Fig 33
Only the outline of the outer edge of the wing is transferred. The radial stitches, their direction indicated by the open arrows, are then worked. Then small stitches are laid over two radial stitches, brickwork fashion and at right angles to the radial stitches. This has been exaggerated for the sake of clarity in the central diagram. As these stitches are tightened the radial stitches will gradually be pulled in opposite directions to form the honeycomb pattern of the wing

· · · · · · · ·

HELEN
STEVENS

pattern will appear (see Fig 33). This honeycombing conveys well the structure of the wing, but the iridescent sheen has yet to be achieved. Seek out any type of specialist thread which contains a strand of cellophane or clear plastic running through it. Separate this out of the main thread and overlay it, radially, across the wings using long even stitches. This will not be visible normally, but when the light catches it, it will shimmer like the membrane on a real wing.

Damselflies are more delicately built than their larger cousins. Their flight is less bold, with a weaker, fluttering character. The banded demoiselle is among the largest of the breed – over 60mm (nearly 2^1/3in) in wingspan – and certainly the prettiest. A different technique may be used to render these dancing, capricious beauties. The banded demoiselle is shown to the left in Plate 42, in flight and at a slight angle so the wings are asymmetrical. As with the dragonfly's wings, draw and transfer only the outline of the wing, and, using the finest thread available, work a series of long radiating stitches from body to wing tip – but much closer together. Then, in the contrasting blue, work the 'bands' by interspersing shorter straight stitches in the appropriate places. The bodies of damselflies are much slighter than those of the dragons. Some are as thin as needles, and may be worked simply in straight stitch, with the addition of a 'band' of gold thread in places where the abdomen narrows further.

Along the river, the poor mayfly is everybody's favourite lunch. It is preyed upon by other flying insects, attacked from below by fish (especially trout, for whom fishermen make false mayflies) and scooped up by martins, swifts, swallows and water wagtails (Plate 39). Thousands of mayflies hatch over a small stretch of water each morning and within twenty-four hours most of them are dead, either eaten or just exhausted because they have no facilities for taking in nutrition. But the mayfly is a vastly decorative insect, and small enough to slip into even a tiny waterstudy. Its wings can be worked exactly as the wings of bees. Its most distinctive and attractive feature is its three long tail filaments, which can be worked as loose straight stitches (take care not to draw them too tightly onto the background fabric).

Plates 39-42 all contain water, and the fluidity of water is difficult to capture in an immobile medium. In painting, only the greatest of the Masters capture it with any degree of reality. As a general rule for embroidery, the principle of 'the less, the more' is a good one to adopt. It is better to suggest a stream's continuation into the distance rather than to extend the sewing too far (Plate 40a). It is better to understate the ripples on the surface as a fish rises (Plate 40) and to concentrate upon reflections rather than the quality of the water itself in a broader study (Plate 39). Experiment with the addition of silver metallic threads. Keep stitches straight, attempting to suggest wavelets and ripples with gradation of colour, rather than direction. Of course there is fun to be had, too! Tiny droplets of spray flicked from a fish's tail or dripping from the rump of a recently submerged kingfisher can be easily depicted by a teardrop shape lightly infilled with silver thread.

Fig 34 △
The yellow flag iris is a perfect companion to almost any watery subject. Worked on black it is an excellent exercise in voiding. Every solid line (with the exception of the outer edges) must be carefully voided

◁ PLATE 42
The dramatic pink flowers of the flowering rush (Butomus umbellatus) are dark veined with purple (shooting stitch) petals off-set by deep maroon sepals. The rush's elegant shape and dramatic colour lend themselves particularly well to work on a black background, where the addition of small touches of gold metallic thread adds to the overall impact. Embroidery shown life size: 24.25 x 19.75cm (9^1/2 x 7^3/4in)

THE PILOT AND THE LADY

The beautiful swallowtail butterfly, christened the 'purple pilot' by World War II airmen, is now extremely rare and confined to small stretches of the Norfolk Broads. The thrill of seeing a swallowtail, one of Britain's biggest butterflies with a wingspan of just under 10cm (almost 4in) is unforgettable.

The best way to describe the elaborate wing patterns of the swallowtail (Plate 43) is as a series of arrow-head devices, all pointing towards the body of the insect. Together with the few scimitar-shaped blobs on the upper wings, these features must be worked first in yellow and lilac. The rest of the brightly coloured wing must then be filled in, blending the shapes and flow of the stitches as closely as possible. The two distinctive 'eye-spots' on the lower wings should also be worked in advance of the rest of the patterning, and then merged.

The exquisite Camberwell beauty butterfly has a wingspan of 6.5cm (almost 3in) and its wings have a quality of crushed velvet, edged with black banding dotted with blue and edged again with a pale creamy lace-like border. This patterning suggested the clothes of a widow just emerging from deep mourning, when etiquette allowed the first additions of lace and decoration, hence the butterfly's country names: white petticoat, lady's mourning cloak and the merry widow.

PLATE 43 ▷

The swallowtail butterfly (Papilio machaon) *is protected in the United Kingdom but despite attempts to reintroduce it to various habitats from which it has become extinct, it has remained stubbornly unco-operative. Ironically, whilst man has been responsible for its decline through the drainage of fens and management of waterways, he was also responsible for its primary habitat, the man-made Broads, excavated in the middle ages for peat and now a favourite holiday location.*

The fen violet (Viola stagnina) *is a pale, watery relative of the headily perfumed sweet violet. Its delicately patterned face, and languid, drooping buds are uncomplicated and make a perfect foil for the intricate designs of the swallowtail 9 x 9cm (3¹/₂ x 3¹/₂in)*

◁ PLATE 44

The more restrained wing patterns of the Camberwell beauty (Nymphalis antiopa) are perfect subjects for the practice of radial stitching, dalmatian-dog and merging techniques. The overall simplicity of the butterfly can be lifted by the inclusion of a more complicated companion plant, in this case the lady's smock, also known as 'milkmaid' or the cuckoo flower. Tradition holds that anyone picking the lady's smock will be bitten by an adder! 9 x 9cm (3½ x 3½in)

PLATE 45 \

Occasionally it is fun to work a piece in a completely original format. This tiny miniature is small enough to lie in the palm of your hand, and yet many of the features discussed in this chapter have been included: the irises, the meandering river, the detailed tree. Never be afraid to experiment with new ideas. Embroidery can be as flexible as your imagination 6.5 x 8.5cm (2½ x 3¼in)

The bodies of both of these large butterflies, the swallowtail and Camberwell beauty, should be worked in such a way as to give them the appearance of flexibility. The head and thorax is worked by infilling the appropriate field with straight stitching, but the 'segments' of the abdomen must be worked in a series of small sections, each separated by a narrow line of voiding. Most butterflies have quite distinctive prominent eyes. These may be worked as very tiny knots, often in a contrasting but appropriate colour, kept close to the sides of the head. With the exception of very small butterflies, such as the various blues (for which it is better to work all sections of the body with simple straight stitching) this method of working may be adopted universally.

When creating simple designs such as butterflies and flowers together always pay some regard to realism. Camberwell is now an area of Inner London and an impossible home for its namesake despite the proximity of the River Thames. But on the river's upper reaches, where it passes through damp meadows clustered with lady's smock, the Camberwell beauty may still be seen gliding effortlessly from flower to willow.

CHAPTER FIVE

AUTUMN LEAVES

*O leafy yellowness you create for me
A world that was and now is poised above time*

'October'
Patrick Kavanagh

◁ *PLATE 46*

Autumn is revealed by colour, from deep vibrant crimson to delicate golden yellow. The nuthatch (Sitta europaea) *is a bird of deciduous woodlands, parks and gardens. Hazel nuts are a favourite food of the red squirrel* (Sciurus vulgaris)*, and those not eaten will be hidden away. The red squirrel's ear tufts should be worked as a final touch, along with whiskers and the finest tail filaments, in a single strand of the finest silk. Lords and ladies* (Arum maculatum) *produce fine, but extremely poisonous, berries. Unlike holly berries, hips or haws, their core is a dimple rather than a free-standing pip, so they must be worked with particular attention to shadow lines. Use the dimple as the growing point around which to centre radial stitching.*

Embroidery shown life size:
39.5 x 27cm (15^1/2 x 10^1/2in)

PLATE 47
(opposite)

The oak is an integral part of much of the British landscape. The pedunculate oak (Quercus robur) *is one of the most common varieties. The familiar greenish-brown acorns, darkening as they mature and fall, are produced in cups with long stems.*
The ivy (Hedera helix) *was considered extraordinary because it produces two entirely different types of leaves: on flowering shoots the leaves are smooth, whilst on non-flowering stems the edges are deeply lobed with up to five angular points, as shown here.*
The red admiral butterfly, seen in flight, reveals the attractive underside of its wing. Actually quite darkly mottled, artistic licence on a black background allows a freer interpretation whilst still retaining the correct detail. The body of the insect is worked in slim silver metallic thread
29.25 x 35.5cm (11^1/2 x 14in)

WHAT TANGLED WEBS...

As autumn approaches the countryside seems subtly to shift gear, as the overdrive of high summer gives way to a more leisurely pace. For the embroiderer, it is once again time to extend the workbox's palette of colours. Dull greens, old gold, russets, amber, blackberry purple and rose-hip red, and a trip to the woodland will provide inspiration for a picture to capture the glorious disorder of the autumn. After a full season's growth, nature is in a tangle. Vines have entwined like lovers around young saplings; fallen, tattered leaves cover the ground; fruits and half-fruits hang heavy; and still the plants with a long flowering and seeding period bloom and reproduce. Plate 47 was worked from a rough sketch made in September. The leaves of the young oak sapling (probably of about two years' growth) had turned early, blackberries were attracting fruit flies and other insects and a young, flexible frond of ivy was already trying to forge an unequal relationship with the oak! It was the untidy imperfections of the scene that made it so appealing.

For all their crumpled edges, the leaves of the oak are essentially simple and centrally veined, but with the coming of autumn we can no longer rely upon two shades of green to be sufficient for colouring. Leaves fade unevenly, often from the edges inward, leaving a streak of green surrounding the vein, or becoming much more weather beaten on one side than the other. On a summer leaf a single strata of stitches is sufficient to describe the field of colour on either side of the vein, but in autumn it may be necessary to extend this to two strata. Remember that the stitches must merge together smoothly, their direction sloping towards the extended 'growing point' and follow the same rules as outlined for double-strata radial stitching on large-petalled flowers.

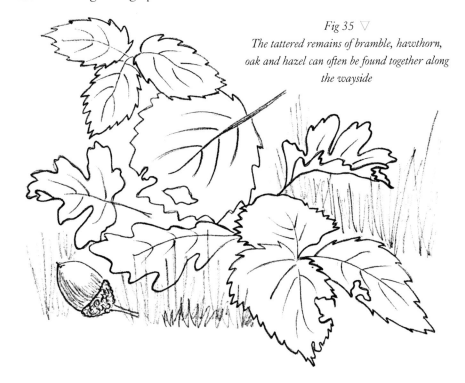

Fig 35 ▽
The tattered remains of bramble, hawthorn, oak and hazel can often be found together along the wayside

HELEN
STEVENS

Fig 36

*Remember that a twining stem such as ivy will
appear to be passing before and behind the 'host'
alternately. It may be sketched initially as a
continuous line, the sections behind the stem
being removed before the design is transferred*

Imperfect fallen leaves are fun too. Leave a ragged hole within the whole
leaf, maintaining the strict directional stitching on either side. If this technique is
attempted on a pale ground, remember to shadow line the underside of the hole.
Experiment with dead leaves and explore the way they lie when they fall. Drained
of their summer sap, they remain crisp, their edges sharp and rigid against the
background.

Ivy is a highly decorative plant. Not only are its leaves beautifully shaped,
but it forms itself into such pleasing curves and contours that it simply begs to be
re-created through embroidery. The sinuous climbing of the main stem can be
conveyed through stem stitch at the top, becoming thicker as the stem becomes
more substantial lower down and gradually metamorphosising into a slim satin (or
snake) stitch.

Its tendrils are perfect for the use of couching. The two most basic forms are
surface and underside couching. The best for natural subjects is surface couching
as the main thread lies smoothly on the background fabric, only disappearing
where the subject disappears behind another feature. Couching is a wonderfully
satisfying technique. In this case it is worked with two needles, one of which must
have an eye large enough to accept the gold thread, which should not be so thick
as to damage the background fabric or be difficult to pull through to the back of
the work. At first it is a good idea to make a detailed sketch of the entwining to be
achieved (see Fig 36) because on a fine fabric you may not wish to transfer the
actual pattern line onto the background in case it is too thick to be covered.
By referring to this sketch you will be able to keep track of where the thread
should disappear and emerge behind other features of the work.

Begin each tendril at its base where it splits from the main stem then bring
your gold thread out smoothly at the junction point. Your second needle, threaded
with a fine couching thread, should be about 2mm (¹/₈in) below it. Lay the gold
thread and catch it down with a tiny stitch. Repeat the process along the length of
the desired tendril, bringing the gold thread through to the back of the work only
when the line is completed. Where it appears to coil around a feature such as the
dandelion stalk in Plate 48, couch right over the top of the other feature, and take
a stitch behind it where necessary to emerge in the correct position to continue.
Keep a close eye on your sketch while working.

< *PLATE 48*
(detail of Plate 47)
In this detail of Plate 47, the realistic use of
couching to depict coiling ivy is more
easily examined. For the sake of continuity of
design, the same gold thread has been used to
create the veining in the ivy leaves Actual
dimensions of section shown:
12.75 x 12.75cm (5 x 5in)

Plate 48 also shows a dandelion clock in greater detail than we have seen before. The dandelion is a wonderful plant, for all its commonplace familiarity. Every part of it is attractive, from bud and leaf to flower and seed head. To understand the dandelion clock, whether tattered as shown here, or more nearly complete (see Plates 1 and 37), it is a good idea to examine its structure at first hand. Dandelions are so widespread that even the most fanatical conservationist could not object to their being picked but keeping those fragile heads intact for detailed sketching is a problem. Help is at hand in the shape of a can of aerosol hairspray, CFC-free of course! On finding a perfect specimen, lightly spray the dandelion clock all over with hairspray before picking. Allow it to dry thoroughly then transport it to the drawing board. A specific section of the downy parachutes may then be removed if desired and the rest of the clock will remain undamaged.

The spherical head of the dandelion clock can be drawn very easily by outlining a circle and filling it with tiny radial stars. The number of these necessary to fill the circle will give you the number of tiny parachutes of embroidery you must work, but it is not a good idea to transfer the total sketch onto the fabric as the fine thread needed to convey the ethereal quality of the parachutes will not be thick enough to cover the background pigment. When transferring the design, impress

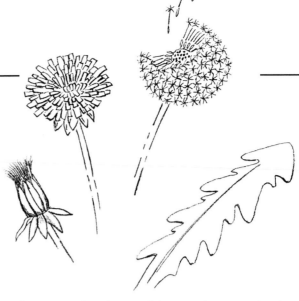

Fig 37 △
Every part of the common dandelion is attractive: the seed head on the point of opening, the flower, the full-blown clock, a mature leaf

only the 'dot' at the centre of each star giving you its respective location on the dandelion head. Then work each parachute or star in a series of fine straight radial stitches, gradually building up the whole.

Where a section of the clock has been blown away, this may reveal the long necks of neighbouring parachutes, or it may leave a hole big enough to uncover part of the core at the centre of the clock and the minute seeds themselves. The core is built up by creating the impression of a sphere, or hemisphere, by the use of tiny random seed stitches close together. The seeds are made by slightly larger seed stitches, radiating from the core. (See Fig 37.)

PLATE 49 ▷
The difference between the narrow-bordered bee hawkmoth (Hemaris tityus) *shown here, and the broad-bordered bee hawkmoth* (Hemaris fuciformis) *shown in Plate 47 is explained by their names. Both insects are day flying, and if you are able to grow rhododendrons in your garden you may well be able to attract them as models. Their wings, in common with the hummingbird hawkmoth, beat so quickly that they become a blur and can only be fully enjoyed when the insects rest in the sun, usually close to a favourite food plant. The delicate flowers of the raspberry* (Rubus idaeus) *are much less showy than the pinker blooms of the blackberry, but their slender sepals, (about the same length or longer than the petals) make them an attractive device in embroidery. The backward curving thorns, less pronounced than those of the bramble, must be worked in a fine thread*
10.25 x 10.25cm (4 x 4in)

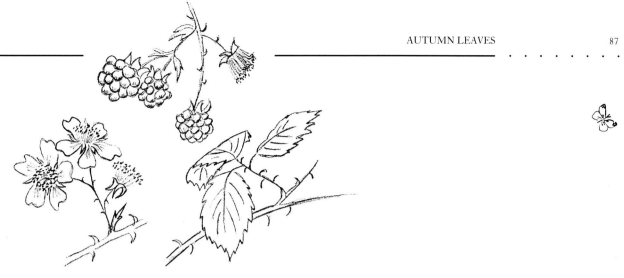

Who can resist the pleasing shape and colour of the blackberry as a subject for embroidery? There are no fewer than two thousand varieties of bramble, each varying slightly from the next, so the leaf and flower of a blackberry bush in one part of the country may appear quite different from those of a bush in another area. The fruits themselves remain fairly uniform, however. The bramble's close cousin, the raspberry, shares many of its characteristics (Plate 49). Wild raspberries have a slightly earlier flowering time than blackberries but they retain their fruiting period until long after their cultivated cousins, so it is possible in sheltered places to find the pretty sight of both side by side.

Blackberries and raspberries may be worked similarly. Each of the many segments which cluster together to make a single 'berry' must be treated individually, and worked as a separate little sphere. Many of the segments are partly hidden by their companions and reveal themselves only as half-moons or scimitar shapes. Both blackberries and raspberries often appear to have a slight 'bloom' over the fruit, bluish in the case of blackberries. Whilst this is almost impossible to capture as a sheen, it can be suggested by using two different shades together, for instance, purple and black. Tiny filaments and specks of a pollen-like substance are also to be found caught between the closely abutted segments of the fruit. This can be indicated by very fine seed stitches randomly interspersed in an appropriate colour.

△ Fig 38
The blackberry: berries and immature fruiting head, leaves and blossoms

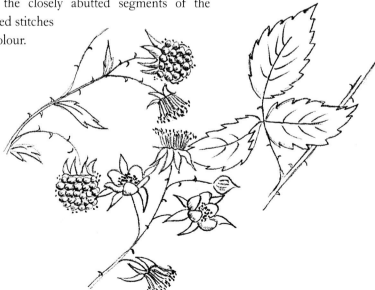

Fig 39 ▷
The raspberry. Tiny specks and filaments which cling to the fruit are too small to be transferred onto fabric and must be added freehand at the time of embroidery

Bee hawkmoths are so called because of their obvious similarity to the larger species of bees. They favour the type of open woodland clearing in which wild raspberries grow undisturbed. They are usually in flight from late spring to midsummer, but in warm years may survive somewhat longer. Their amazingly complex wings have the same transparent quality as those of the dragonfly and damselfly and it is effective to work them over the top of some other feature creating a three-dimensional effect with the background object showing through the insect's wing. Their stumpy little bodies are almost too plump to reveal any segmentation, but the banding of the lower body can be suggested by running a couple of courses of 'laddering' lightly through the overlying stitches, and then pulling the ladder stitches down slightly so that they appear to follow the contour of the body.

A PRICKLY QUESTION

Many of the most prevalent shapes in nature are not easy to capture with recognised embroidery techniques. Indeed, most of the commonly identifiable stitches, however close their names may appear to bring them to nature (lazy daisy is a perfect example), are obtrusive. It is the stitch which catches the eye and not the subject matter which it is intended to convey. As we begin to approach the more

PLATE 50 ▷
Symbol of Scotland for centuries, the Scottish thistle (Onopordon acanthium) *is also a valuable food plant for many butterflies, including the migratory painted lady* (Cynthia cardui), *which is particularly fond of the narrow, nectar-filled florets. Painted ladies are swift, strong flyers, often travelling at up to 15kph (10mph) during their migration from southern Europe and North Africa. Early arrivals in May and June produce a second generation which are on the wing in September and October and provide ideal autumn subjects for sketching, their distinctive red 'eyes' being a primary feature of the wing pattern. Where the butterfly's lower wing lightens gradually towards its body, try lightening the shade of embroidery by mixing similar but paler shades in the same needle 9 x 9.5cm (3¹/₂ x 3³/₄in)*

complicated designs suggested by the countryside, we must turn away from any preconceived ideas of what embroidery can achieve and rely upon our own ingenuity to create the desired effect.

The beautiful but complex Scottish thistle is a case in point. It is made up of a number of features, all of which appear at first glance to be almost impossible to render realistically. The trick is to break the plant down into its component parts and treat each separately. There is no denying that the thistle is a difficult subject – even its sketch presents problems. It is made up of a series of spine-tipped bracts radiating from a spherical body, like the prickles on a sea urchin. (If all else fails, a good book on heraldry will provide stylised thistles for you to adapt.)

First, sketch a circle, then add a series of long tapering arrow heads, remembering that those pointing towards you will reflex (see Fig 40). Roughly sketch in the long, whisker-like florets. Decide upon the curve of the stem and leaves and rough this in, later adding the random deeply toothed prickles. Transfer the design onto the fabric, omitting any very fine details, and work the globe first. Here we come into contact with chevron stitch, which will solve many a prickly problem. Treat each prickle independently (with a shadow line) and take a long stitch on the opposite side to the shadow. Coming to the shadow side, take another long stitch, worked at an angle to meet the first. If your prickle has been sketched slimly enough this should fill the motif. If not, take a third stitch to fill in the space in the middle, but do not extend beyond the stitches already taken. Treat all the prickles in the same way, and a three-dimensional sphere will miraculously appear. Work down the length of the stem and leaf in *opus plumarium*, changing direction smoothly as necessary. Using as fine a thread as possible, work the long straight filaments of the flower head. Finally, with a similarly fine thread, work a single long straight stitch right through every prickle to create a wicked looking spine. Needless to say, colour matching is all important for this type of study, so choose your greens carefully. Thistles tend to have a bluish bloom about them (some even have a downy substance which makes the green appear dull and matt in finish) so try mixing colours in your needle.

Chevron stitch may be used to describe almost any type of prickle, and may be adapted as necessary. The foliage of the common juniper (Plate 51) is made up

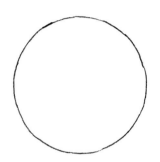

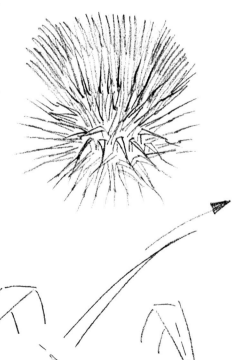

Fig 40 ▷

A rough circle decides the size of the 'globe' for the thistle's head. (Later this can be omitted.) The long, tapering spines are added, in a multitude of directions as shown below. Finally, the wicked, very fine prickle is added in the direction of the spine, as indicated by the dotted line on the spine

PLATE 51 >

The tiny goldcrest (Regulus regulus) *is only
9cm (3¹/₂in) from beak to tail, and spends most
of its time in coniferous trees, seeking out its diet
of insects and their larvae. Among the festive
decorations of the juniper tree, its distinctive
gold and green markings give it a toy-town air,
but it is quite aggressive with its neighbours,
entering into hot rivalry with firecrests. (It is
however quite indifferent to man, and will
continue to search for food in a tree which is
being pruned!) The compact shape may be
begun as a triangle, and then rounded off to
produce head, body and tail (Fig 41)*
10.25 x 10.25cm (4 x 4in)

Fig 41 ∧

*As we become familiar with the positioning of
subject matter, we can slip a little bird in
among the foliage with ease. This presents a
much more attractive and 'finished' design
than, for instance the chaffinch in Fig 21*

of sharp-pointed needles, which spread out from their stems in thickly placed whorls of three. Grey-green in colour, they are not as wickedly spined as thistles, so the angle of the chevron stitch is less acute to produce a gentler-tipped result. For similar reasons the final long thin spines of the thistle are omitted.

The sharply delineated, stark shape of chevron stitching creates satisfying contrasts with other elements of a design. The female cones of the juniper, which take up to three years to reach maturity, look like perfectly spherical berries. At first green, and then ripening gradually through dull blue into purple-black they look for all the world like Christmas tree decorations nestling among the needles. As they have such a long ripening period cones may well appear at different stages of maturity on the same tree, compounding this effect.

On a black background, chevron stitching is equally effective in its various forms (Plate 52). So far, we have dealt with plant prickles: the hedgehog is another matter. Anyone who has had the privilege of meeting a hedgehog face to face (young ones can be quite bold and seem to feel that the obligation to roll up into the customary ball is an anti-social attitude inflicted upon them by their elders) will remember the contrast between the rigid spines and delightfully soft and fluffy underside fur. A hedgehog's face, belly and legs are all covered with this greyish golden-brown fur, and only the upper body has prickles, themselves adapted hairs. There is a strong muscle, the orbicularis, which lies just beneath the skin of the animal's back and neck. This contracts to make the spines rise and encircle the whole animal as it curls up. Because this muscle extends the length of the body and is flexible, the prickles rarely lie at a completely uniform angle, but move with the contours of the hedgehog's body. Just above the neck they may stand up, but on the back they lie flatter and at the side, where they join the soft underbelly fur, they droop down slightly.

To complicate matters further, each spine is not a uniform colour, but is banded. In embroidery, this effect can be achieved by a mixture of chevron and ticking. The upper surface of the spine should be worked in pale grey, the lower in a darker shade and the long, needle-like prickle through the centre (similar to the thistle's wicked point, but slightly shorter) should be worked with a third shade to create the ticking effect, just as in the plumage of a bird.

Unlike the dog rose, both the delicate burnet rose and the soft-leaved rose have straight slender prickles, not the claw-like thorns of their relatives. These too can be conveyed through chevron stitching though working with a finer thread produces a slimmer and more elegant shape. The longer the stitches, the more acute the angle, the more dangerous is the prickle created.

PLATE 52 ∨

Although occasionally persecuted by gamekeepers for the few eggs they might eat, and eaten themselves, tradition says, by gypsies, the hedgehog (Erinaceus europaeus) *and man lived together largely in harmony – until the coming of the motorcar. Campaigns have been launched to make motorists 'hedgehog conscious' and a number of hedgehog hospitals have sprung up to cater for accident victims, much to the credit of their primarily volunteer workforce. Also sometimes known as land urchins, baby hedgehogs are, of course, piglets, and are born with soft white prickles which they moult to be replaced by darker, sharper spines. By four to six weeks they are weaned and begin their life-long diet of insects, worms and snails* 18 x 9cm (7 x 3½in)

HELEN
STEVENS

◁ *Fig 42*
The classical acanthus motif

FAIRY RINGS

Perhaps because they have a tendency to spring into life stealthily in dark secretive places fungi seem to be regarded with a certain amount of suspicion. In the British Isles there are over three thousand species of large-bodied fungi alone, yet only about twenty of them are seriously poisonous (admittedly four fatally so!) and many of them are astonishingly beautiful, crying out to be included in countryside art. Nature has evolved the strategy of warning small hungry creatures that a substance is poisonous by adopting the universal 'red is dangerous' signal, as with the notorious fly agaric (Plate 54). Then she contradicted herself by making rose hips, equally red and startling, an ideal meal for small creatures building up a reserve of fat for the long winter's hibernation. It is part of the magic of the countryside that these confused signals can be interpreted at all by its inhabitants, but when you are a mouse, and need to eat a substantial portion of your own body weight each day just to survive, such knowledge comes with the territory!

PLATE 53 (opposite)
A study using the classical acanthus motif and inspired by eighteenth-century designs. The acanthus is a real, thistle-like plant, full of prickles and spines, whose natural characteristics have been all but forgotten in its long life as a stylised motif. The acanthus motif is found among the earliest fragments of surviving embroidery from Scandinavian ship burials, and it is also the subject of the first literary allusion to embroidery design; Virgil records that Helen of Troy's gown was embroidered with a motif of acanthus. According to legend, a Greek architect, Callimachos, was visiting the grave of a bride who died on the eve of her wedding. Gifts and flowers had been laid alongside the tomb, forcing the leaves of a nearby acanthus backwards into a decorative shape. He adapted the motif to fit the pillars of a temple he was building at Corinth – and the Corinthian column was born. Before long, the elegant backward sweep of the acanthus had been adopted by artists and craftsmen working in every field from metalwork to weaving. It is a useful and attractive device to include in any formal embroidery design
19 x 23cm (7$\frac{1}{2}$ x 9in)

HELEN STEVENS

◁ *PLATE 54*
The infamous fly agaric (Amanita muscaria), *one of the few common poisonous toadstools, is quite unmistakable. For this study, the warts on the larger toadstool have been worked in dalmatian dog, and those on the smaller are in right-angled dalmation dog, that is the direction of the stitches are at variance with the direction of the surrounding* opus plumarium
9 x 9.5cm (3$\frac{1}{2}$ x 3$\frac{3}{4}$in)

The cap of the fly agaric appears to be covered with white warts. These are actually the remains of the tissue which covered the toadstool in its button stage and they gradually disappear as the fungus grows larger and flattens into a concave saucer shape. These may be approached, either with the dalmatian-dog technique or superimposed on top (for once, the feature is a surface one and not part of a single plane). In either case, a complete 360° disc must be completed in radial stitching to convey the dipped surface of the cap. The gills of the toadstool beneath the cap should be worked in a series of straight stitches, following the direction of the original.

The blusher (Plate 55) reverses this process. It has a convex cap (still ornamented with warts), and, seen from an angle slightly below the level of the cap, it is the gills which must radiate from a central core. Both fungi have a ring (the remains of the skin of the stem, peeling backwards) which hangs down like a

PLATE 55 ▷

The blusher fungus (Amanita rubescens) *is edible, but it is best avoided because of its close resemblance to a highly poisonous species. Insects invade many fungi, and older specimens are often riddled with tiny holes where larvae have fed. An effective trick to add interest to a picture is to create tiny 'fruit flies' (impossible to identify in any textbook) which can be worked easily with two caught-down looped stitches and a few random straight stitches. Placed haphazardly in a design, they can draw the eye from one important feature to the next (see Fig 43)* 10.5 x 13cm (4 x 5in)

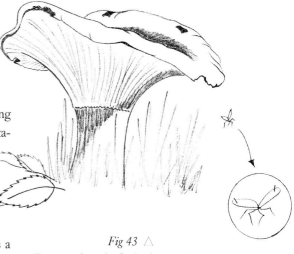

short skirt. Cleverly used, voiding can create the impression of this feature encircling the stems of the plants. The endless variety of fungi allows for fun and experimentation. Try taking the three-dimensional concave shape to extremes with *Lactarius turpis* – its correct common name is 'the ugly one' (Fig 43), or delicate fairy ring toadstools such as the delightfully named 'little Japanese umbrella' (Fig 44).

Anyone who lives in the country will at some time have been visited indoors by outdoor mice! Whilst the house mouse is generally unwelcome it is a hard-hearted individual who resorts to the mouse trap when confronted with a wood or field mouse. The wood mouse's natural foodstuffs are seeds, berries, nuts and small invertebrates; and he is himself an important element in the food chain, being prey for owls and other raptors.

Opus plumarium is as effective for fur as it is for feathers. First work the eye and any other facial features which need to be emphasised, such as the nose, and use these as the 'core' from which to radiate your stitches. Around the nose and the mouth of the mouse are puffy cheek areas often speckled where the whiskers emerge. These areas give the creature character, so work them carefully, mixing colours (especially white) in the needle, if necessary. Afterwards, superimpose the speckles with tiny seed stitches (they are too small to be created by dalmatian-dog technique). When the whole animal is finished add long whiskers springing from the cheeks and above the eyes, and bring the eye to instant life by adding a white highlight.

AUTUMN LANDSCAPES

Plate 56 shows the rolling landscape of Suffolk in the late autumn. The fields are harvested and the bales of straw have been collected and removed for winter use. In the hedgerow, the many shades of autumn are overtaking the varied greens of summer, whilst species with long flowering seasons make a showy display (mallows, poppies, scentless mayweed, St John's wort). Shrubs which flowered earlier in the year are now fruiting; the blackberries still hang on their runners and where the May blossom rioted in the spring the haws are now thickly clustered. At this time, trees in the middle distance appear to thin out, letting more light through their foliage, but on the far skyline they still appear dense, and a strong infill of straight stitching conveys their solidity. In the forefront of the hedgerow a hawthorn tree has many different shades of darkening leaf and bright bunches of fruit, worked in groups of red stitches.

Where once country roads were dusty affairs in the summer, mired with mud in the winter, most are now metalled. The blue-grey surface of a made-up road is not unattractive, nor is it uniform. Puddles have darkened the outer edges, and in places grass grows through the surface where it meets the verge. Don't be afraid to convey great sweeps of arable fields by long, bold stitching. From a distance a harvested field looks stark. Be careful not to overstate the sky. In embroidery we find once again that the principle of 'the less, the more' is infinitely more expressive.

Fig 43 △
Fungi rarely make the focal point of a picture, but they are useful as added interest, and stand obligingly still be sketched. A tiny, impressionistic 'fruit fly', can be suggested by two looped stitches, caught down lightly so that their loops are loose on the background fabric, with a few jointed legs indicated by random straight stitches. The flies should not really exceed about 2-3mm, (^{1}/8in), in height or they will lose spontaneity and become clumsy

Fig 44 △
Little Japanese umbrellas and fairy-ring champignons

PLATE 56 >
Autumn in Suffolk Embroidery shown life
size: 30.5 x 18.5cm (12 x 7¹/₄in)

CHAPTER SIX

THE VANISHING HEATH

Stripped are the great sun-clouding planes:
And the dark pines, their own revealing,
Let in the needles of the noon.

'Autumn'
Roy Campbell

PLATE 58 ▽

The male kestrel (Falco tinnunculus) *has a
dramatic blue-grey head and tail. In flight, on
the point of stooping for its prey, the kestrel has
every feather extended, and every part of the
bird must be worked in the appropriate
manner. The order of working feathers must be
observed (refer to the kingfisher in flight on
page 69), the barring of the tail must merge
smoothly, yet distinctively, and the ticking must
be just the right angle.*
13.5 x 18.5cm (5¹/₄ x 7¹/₄in)

AS FAR AS THE EYE CAN SEE

Authors have always found the greatness of moor and heath inspirational, and in the last century in particular, when life elsewhere was beginning to change so quickly, the vast and apparently inviolate heathlands provided the settings for dramatic novels by authors such as Emily Brontë and Thomas Hardy. Alas, now we know that the moors were not indestructible. Hardy's Egdon Heath has almost completely disappeared taking with it its bird, animal and butterfly populations.

An open landscape of rolling plains offers an altogether different aspect from any form of cultivated countryside, and in embroidery must be approached accordingly. In an arable setting the contours of the landscape are often broken up by hedgerows and trees, but the moor's only lines may be the contours of the hills and shallow valleys (see Plate 57).

The gentle dip and rise of a dale may be clothed with deep-purple and green patches of heather, perhaps threaded with footpaths and sheep tracks, depicted by very fine close seed stitches. On the other side, green ferns or later in the year, the reddish-brown of bracken may present a more uniform appearance. In this case long, bold stitches may be used across wide areas to suggest a rolling undisturbed expanse of plant life. Where trees appear to separate features of the landscape, they are often stunted, stark against the sky, or partly blasted by harsh winds. They offer scope for achieving some interesting effects. In places branches may be fully leaved with each twig covered with stitches, slightly lighter above and darker beneath. Other areas of the same tree may have 'antlers' of bare branches.

PLATE 57 (page 98–9)
The cliff-top grass, the sheer sides of the cliffs themselves and the beaches below are all worked in cotton or matt silk. By contrast, and to emphasise its reflective quality, the sea is worked in floss silk, the shade darkening almost imperceptibly as it recedes into the distance. The craggy quality of the cliffs is achieved by use of a substantial shadow line, and a darker shade of grey is used to surround this line (particularly beneath it). The same principle is applied to the rocks reaching out into the water. The buzzard (Buteo buteo) is Britain's most common large bird of prey. Small heathland plants and shrubs such as the small yellow-stemmed furze (Ulex minor) and the pink-flowered clumps of thrift (Armeria maritima) cling like sea urchins to the rocks.
Embroidery shown life size:
41 x 27cm (16 x 10½in)

◁ *PLATE 59*
Water voles (Arvicola terrestris) are often called water rats, but they are only distantly related, and prefer to live in clean water, undisturbed by man.
To create the effect of the shallow river's edge, it is necessary to work from a sketch which has already captured the correct perspective (see Fig 51). Work the perpendicular stitches first, then surmount them by horizontal straight stitches to create the grassy upper bank, on which small tussocks of grass and other plants may be superimposed. Work the water last of all, allowing it to 'lap' up over the base of the perpendicular stitches. Remember that the water which is close to the bank will appear darker where it is overshadowed, creating an impression of reflection
12.75 x 9.5cm (5 x 3¾in)

Fig 45 △

The stark outline of a Scots pine against the sky is typical of the windswept heath. Rough in only the outline of the outermost sections of needles. Then use tiny seed stitches to build up the rest of the foliage almost randomly within the framework of the long straight trunk and scrappy, broken branches

Fig 46

Enlarged to create a full embroidery, this sketch would include a detailed study of the bird, together with an impression of the landscape below. Filling the void between the two would lessen the impact of the design

The wind is a dominant feature on the moors. It keeps vegetation and wild-flowers low and in winter whips up great drifts of snow, making food hard to find. However, it is the ally of birds of prey, notably the kestrel (Plate 58) whose old country name 'windhover' aptly suggests the partnership. Wings outstretched and facing into the wind, the kestrel hovers, its head motionless and eyes scanning the ground for prey. Many raptors are almost entirely confined to moorland as their habitats have been destroyed, but fortunately the kestrel has learned to live in harmony with many of man's innovations. Wide grassy motorway verges have created 'false moorlands' and, thanks to a decrease in poison-based pest controls, the kestrel is on the increase. The kestrel's telescopic eyesight enables it to spot prey from over a hundred feet above ground. Once the prey has been seen the kestrel plummets downward, in spectacular fashion, feet extended to grab the unfortunate victim.

Plates 58 and 59 are details from the same large study of predator and prey (though in this case the water vole has every chance to escape into the little heath-land rill which is its home). In the original study these two features are separated by a large expanse of open fabric, unencumbered by any form of decoration. If we refer back to other pictures, such as Plates 30 and 40, we can see just how important space can be. An easy mistake in embroidery design is to feel that every part of the canvas must be crammed with activity. On the contrary, the spaces left can be as important as the features themselves. They balance the picture, direct the eye and emphasise the subject matter. The markings of the kestrel are complicated and 'busy'. The water vole is surrounded by detail which demands the viewer's attention: gorse, grasses, river's edge and water. There is a great deal to look at in these two features alone. More embroidery would only confuse the eye. The sketch in Fig 46 shows a similar scene in its original format.

< PLATE 60
The common ragwort (Senecio jacobaea) *is something of a Cinderella among plants. Anathema to some (it is the cause of much hay fever), it is to be found on barren areas of heath and breckland, and often on waste sites, but it is the food plant of one of the most spectacular of all day-flying moths, the cinnabar* (Tyria jacobaeae). *On a black background, the bright buttery yellow of the flower is seen to its best advantage. The design is simplified by using only one or two of the heads rather than a mass of small florets. The centre of each flower, picked out with seed stitches in gold metallic thread, makes a tiny, round pin cushion, and the veining of the leaves can be thrown into relief by applying the same gold thread, held down by a green/gold couching thread. With careful positioning of the moths, one of nature's understudies can become a star!*
9 x 9.5cm (3$^{1}/_{2}$ x 3$^{3}/_{4}$in)

HEATHLAND SHRUBS

Greens, yellow, purples and browns are the colours of the heath, and of these none are more striking than the golden-yellow masses of gorse and broom. We have explored at length the various methods of capturing a plant's 'character' both in close up and in the distance, but there are times when it is useful to be able to show the plant occupying the middle ground (see Plates 59 & 62). It is important

Figs 47 and 48
Fig 47 shows the basic outline of the broom, its elegant, curving branches ready to be clothed with an impression of foliage (Fig 48). Without colour, these sketches appear bland, but they will soon be brought to life by green and yellow stitching

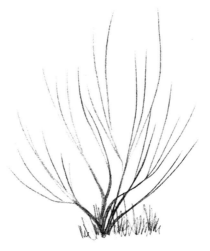

PLATE 61 >

As recently as 1945 the silver-studded blue
(Plebejus argus) was so common that it was
reported to have been sighted by pilots in thick
swarms. Alas, since World War II vast tracts
of heath have been turned into farmland,
destroying this butterfly's natural food plants.
The females are dull and brownish and the
males are more showy, but on both sexes the
tips on the outer edges of the wings are created
by very narrow strata of radiating opus
plumarium 11.5 x 20.5cm (4¹/₂ x 8in)

to strike a happy balance between fine detail and impressionism so that the essential features are conveyed without overcomplicating the stitching. In the same way as when we began landscape interpretation, observation is the key. Look out of the window at a shrub an appropriate distance away. Sketch firstly the overall shape, then rough in an impression of the details (see Figs 47 & 48).

When transferring the design onto fabric you may prefer to outline just the basic shape, or transfer the whole design. Either way, use a fine thread for the embroidery so that as many of the details as possible can be included without over-bunching the stitches. Leave out any irrelevant details, including, for once, the shadow line. In the mid-distance light and shade can be described by varying the colours used: in Plate 59 spines and prickles pointing upwards (where they are not shadowed by a feature above them) are worked in a lighter shade than those pointing down. Remember your imaginary light source and let it do the job for you. The flowers of gorse often have a reddish tinge on their inner lips. At a distance this detail would not be clear but it still needs to be suggested by a single stitch accurately placed. Do not include this in every flower as regimentated detail can begin to look very unrealistic.

Often found alongside gorse is broom, *planta-de-genista* (adopted by the Plantagenet dynasty of English kings). Broom is another member of the pea family, and presents us with a whole new range of shapes (Plate 61). Its branches curve like a tightly strung bow and are just as flexible, but they cannot be worked smoothly in stem stitch as they are constantly interrupted along their length by small leaves. It is better to begin with the leaves (they are so small that we can justify this exception to the usual rule) and then fill the stem in around them. The shape of the flowers must be worked in techniques suggested by the lessons of the honeysuckle study. The curve of the upper petals must be allowed to form naturally as the stitches are worked firstly towards and then away from the growing point. The flower's style and stamens burst out of its 'mouth' like little fireworks.

However, it is in the fruiting body of the broom, the pod, that an entirely new challenge comes to light. The calyx which sheathed the stamens and style during flowering is the base of the pod, which grows in a decided curve and is continued by the long style, which is retained at the apex of the pod. A long whiskered membrane falls like a curtain to protect the calyx when small, and remains like an apron hanging from the calyx as it gets bigger. The first stitches must create the shadow line, outlining the overall shape of the pod. Then, beginning at the apex of the long style, work it in very fine stem stitch. When this reaches the point at which it joins the pod, expand the technique into snake stitch and work up towards the calyx following the curve of the pod. Work the small visible area of the other side of the pod using the opposite angle principle employed with leaves and petals. Finally, work the whiskered apron in the same way, allowing the angle of stem stitch for each whisker to blend smoothly with the broader stitching at the top of the pod. This order of working is noted in Fig 49.

The restharrow is a relative of both the gorse and broom, its pretty purplish-pink flowers giving away its membership of the pea family by their shape (little

Fig 49

The pea pod of the broom is a complicated device (Plate 61 shows similar pods). With a light source from above, practically the whole of the motif requires a shadow line (top), then stem and snake stitch follow the curve of the pod upward in the direction shown (next down). Opposite angle stitching infills the small area to the left of the central join of the pod and finally the whiskered apron completes the motif (bottom)

upturned socks!). It can grow up to more than 60cm (24in) tall and in Plate 62 is shown to the same scale as the gorse previously discussed (Plate 59). Compare the two studies to explore the similarities and differences between the two plants, and note which features have been emphasised or omitted because of perspective. Just as the impression of a receding perspective can be achieved by simplifying elements of the same flower as it falls away into the distance, so a specific 'place' in the mid foreground can be created by this form of interpretation. The water vole and baby rabbit in both scenes are there to show the relative size of the other features, and they have been worked using a very fine thread so that all the details such as whiskers, claws, ears and eye highlight can be included. Using such fine-gauge thread it is difficult to include more than one colour at a time to achieve a merging of colour, so it is necessary to have a wide range of browns, golds and beige.

THE DRY, THE WET AND THE WINDY

Heaths and moorlands, though dwindling, are not confined to any single type of soil or climatic conditions. Moors may consist of dry grassland, wet marshy ground, or windswept areas of cliff and sand dune. Three plants, each completely different in their own right, are perfect to illustrate the diverse plant and insect life of the vanishing heath.

PLATE 62 ▷

Whatever the threat from above, this rabbit's burrow, concealed beneath the restharrow (Ononis repens) *should provide a means of escape. Restharrow may grow either fairly upright (as shown here) or with a more low-lying habit. Its name refers to the tough fibrous roots of the plant, which enforced 'rest' upon a horsedrawn harrow while the hard-pressed farmer had to dig up the plant*
14 x 11.5cm (5¹/2 x 4¹/4in)

◁ *PLATE 63*
The red streaks in the yolk-yellow petals of the
bird's foot trefoil (Lotus corniculatus) *gives a*
clue to this plant's country name of 'bacon-and-
eggs', although it also rejoices in over seventy
other folk names from 'God Almighty's thumb
and finger' to 'Lady's shoes and stockings'.
Whilst chalk-hill blue caterpillars feed on the
plant, it is unlikely that the butterflies pollinate
it: as with many members of the pea family it
relies more upon strong insects such as bees to
force the flower open and reach the pollen and
nectar at its base 10.75 x 7.5cm (4^{1}/4 x 3in)

The grassy upland plains of Wiltshire in southern England are typical of the gently rolling countryside favoured (though not exclusively, for the plant is widespread) by the common bird's foot trefoil (Plate 63). This is yet another member of the pea family which, in open conditions, may grow to about 10cm (4in) high, though when sheltered by other plants it can reach 40cm (16in). It is a food plant of the now rare chalk-hill blue butterfly, which as its name suggests thrives on chalky slopes such as those of Salisbury Plain. The chalk-hill blue is quite different from many other small blue butterflies; the male's wings are much paler, ice-blue above, and the underside of the wing on both sexes is elaborately decorated. The working of the underside of the wing incorporates several techniques combined. (See also the silver-studded blues in Plate 61.)

Initially, the underside of the wing is worked in *opus plumarium*, with the stitches on the upper and lower wings radiating from the body as the supposed 'growing point'. Then shooting stitches are shot outward from the body towards the edge of the wing, extending only as far as the wing pattern suggests. Finally, the tiny spots or studding must be overlaid on top of both. Bearing in mind that these butterflies are being worked at approximately life size, 35mm (just over 1^{1}/4in), the scale is obviously too small to employ the dalmatian-dog technique, and ticking would not create a bold enough effect. We must therefore work tiny seed stitches at an angle of 90° to the original stitching, each stitch only spanning a single thread of the radial *opus plumarium*. Perhaps we should call this technique

Fig 50 ▷
*Motifs taken from the Maaseik textiles
showing trefoil and quatrefoil devices (three-
and four-leaf 'clover' motifs). Also shown
(below right) is a zoomorphic beast surrounded
by indeterminate foliage including reflex trefoils*

Fig 51 △
*Sketchbook design suitable for the working of a
good luck gift?*

'studding' in honour of the silver-studded blues. It is really a much finer version
of the seed stitching used for the wild strawberry. On the upper surface of the
bottom wings of the chalk-hill blue (Plate 63) the grey spots are worked dalmatian-dog fashion. Contrast this with the studding in the same picture and you will
see the very different results of the two methods of working.

Before turning away from the trefoil, it is interesting to recall what an
ancient motif it is in embroidery. As a decorative device it ranks with acanthus and
vine scrolling in its importance, and features extensively in the Maaseik embroideries of the mid Anglo-Saxon period (which were certainly typical of their time,
though they are now unique in their survival).

Grass-of-Parnassus (Plate 65) is not a grass despite its name, but it is typical
of the plants which thrive on wet moorlands and marshy ground. It is common in
Scotland. The delicate white flowers are quite large, up to 2.5cm (1in) across, and
the height of the plant can be anything from 10 to 40cm (4 to 15³/4in). The leaves
are heart shaped, either growing singly on long stalks, or stalkless, growing just

PLATE 64 ▽
Part of the reconstructed Maaseik embroideries, this monogram clearly shows the use of the trefoil device. The embroidery originates from the same workshop as other sections of the Maaseik textiles (see Plate 16), but with its slightly less complex subject matter could have been the work of an apprentice. There is no overtly Christian symbolism in any of the designs, and it would therefore seem unlikely that the quatrefoil devices included in the monogram are intended to be crosses (see Fig 50). Could it be, given the rest of the subject matter on this piece, that they are intended to be 'four-leafed clovers'? The Anglo-Saxons were fond of visual riddles, and it is occasionally fun to follow their example. A design such as that shown in Fig 51 might well include a hidden good luck symbol

Monogram's actual dimensions: 12.75 x 12.75cm (5 x 5in)

PLATE 65 ▷
Starry white grass-of-Parnassus (Parnassia palustris) *was named after Mount Parnassus in Greece, a fitting tribute to this beautiful plant 9 x 10.25cm (3¹/₂ x 4in)*

Fig 52 ▽
The flowers of the mossy saxifrage are delicate and ethereal, and should be worked in a fine gauge of silk. In a design such as this, with the central plant, the butterflies could be replaced by other insects, or a spider's web could be included. The design could even be used as a section of a larger picture with a bird in flight, such as a wagtail, or other species which enjoys the environment of a highland stream. Experiment by using motifs in different ways

under halfway up each flowering stem. This is a simple study, containing relatively few colours, but it contains a number of the most delicate of the techniques which have been discussed. Fig 52 shows the mossy saxifrage, another fragile-looking heathland plant which likes rocky hillsides. This sketch could be translated into embroidery in similar fashion, almost as a 'sampler' of the various techniques and devices with which we have experimented.

The final moorland habitat to explore is that of the rolling, cliff-edged downs leading to the coast. Here grassland gives way to banks of sandy dunes where the yellow lady's bedstraw grows in great drifts of swaying colour. Its flowers are tiny, four-petalled stars clustering tightly on many branched stems, with small single-veined leaves. Lady's bedstraw is the main food plant of the bedstraw hawkmoth (Plate 66) which has predominantly yellow-gold markings offset by two red 'eyes' and thus makes a perfect design companion. Whilst a large study can benefit from the inclusion of a wide range of colours and shades, in a small picture it can be effective to concentrate upon one colour 'theme', in this case gold. In addition to the overall colouring of the study, small touches of gold metallic thread have been included in the centre of each tiny flower, and on the narrow-bordered bee hawkmoth. (A design such as

< *PLATE 66*
Lady's bedstraw (Galium verum) *has a particular association with embroidery; a red dye obtained from its roots was one of the earliest sources of colouring for threads and fabrics. Attempts in recent centuries to cultivate the plant on a widespread basis have failed, however, as the yields proved uneconomically low. The bedstraw hawkmoth* (Hyles gallii) *flies mostly at dusk when it will delicately sip the nectar of this and another plant once widely cultivated for the dyeing of embroidery stuffs, field madder 9 x 9cm (3¹/₂ x 3¹/₂in)*

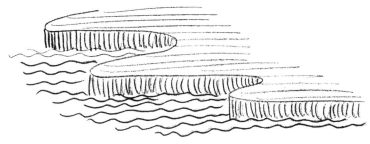

Fig 53 ∨
A shallow river or rill's edge is built up of three planes, as shown in the top diagram. Treated more naturalistically and finally translated into embroidery, the contrast of the directional stitching will suggest and emphasise water, bank and dry land respectively

this might well be a suitable gift for a golden wedding anniversary or similar occasion.)

The windy, often wet moorlands, despite their lonely beauty are teeming with life and inspiration. As Emily Brontë wrote:

> *All is yet the same as when*
> *I roved the heather*
> *Still on those heights*
> *Heath and harebell intone*

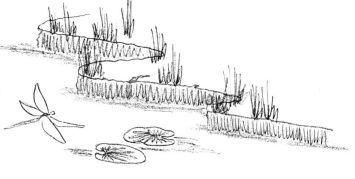

CHAPTER SEVEN

WINTER EVENINGS

Over the land freckled with snow half-thawed
The speculating rooks at their nests cawed
And saw from elm-tops, delicate as flower of grass,
What we below could not see, Winter pass.

'Thaw'
Edward Thomas

A WINTER'S TAIL

In the countryside every season has its own special beauty, none more diverse than the winter. The soft edges and gentle swathes of summer colour are gone, replaced by a cold blue sky and rolling plains of snow with only a suggestion of the features beneath. Or beneath an iron sky the fields lie locked in gun-metal grey, frozen puddles like black mirrors of shisha stitched down by tangles of dead grasses.

Many birds and animals change their appearance with the coming of winter, some even change their names. In severe weather the stoat turns into the creamy white ermine. Where winters are less harsh the stoat's colour change may be partial, but even if it turns fully white, the tip of the tail always remains black (hence the heraldic device of 'ermine', white with a small black motif) (see Fig 54). The ultimate test of *opus plumarium* is to work white on a black background, and the stoat-in-ermine presents this opportunity (see Plate 68). It is essential that stitches lie smoothly, evenly and close together, the sweep of their direction altering as the strata progress from nose to tail, branching off to become legs, feet, individual toes. Voiding is used to differentiate between these features and subdued voiding is used where it is necessary to soften the effect, as where a foreleg crosses in front of the body. It is then possible to make the individual toes appear quite distinct by voiding without the additional softening.

In a detailed study such as this problems present themselves in the most unlikely manner. White whiskers disappear against white fur, and black whiskers disappear when they reach the black background fabric. This can be overcome

◁ *PLATE 67*

The winter countryside offers some surprising images which present a whole new aspect, different from the conventional 'Christmas card' scene. Deciduous trees are bare, but even without a frosting of white they can be starkly beautiful. The delicate twigs of this rowan (Sorbus aucuparia) reveal a structure hidden all summer by its dense foliage. Beneath it the dead stems and heads of last season's cow parsley are the shape of dark snowflakes. The common nettle remains green and lush whilst on many wild rose bushes the leaves hang on stubbornly for months, changing in colour from a sombre dark green to red and crimson with green undertones. Gone are the bright grasses of summer and autumn, but deeper shades and brown bracken-coloured stems still soften the ground. The silky grey catkins of the goat willow begin to emerge in February. The winter aconite (Eranthis hyemalis) with its green frilly collar of leaves is a welcome arrival in January in woodlands and small plantations. A delicate shade of green hides on the underside of the holly's glossy, waxy, dark-green upper surface. The challenge of directional stitching is here taken to its limit.

The common dormouse (Muscardinus avellanarius) sleeps through the winter, rolled into a tight ball in a warm nest of leaves and grasses. Above him, the barren strawberry (Potentilla sterilis) may just still be in bloom when he wakes.
Embroidery shown life size:
41 x 27cm (16 x 10¹/₂in)

PLATE 68 ▷

Though the stoat and the weasel are so similar as to be often confused, the poor weasel became associated with an underhanded personality, while the stoat (Mustela erminea), at least in ermine, became a symbol of purity. In a famous portrait of Elizabeth I it represents virginity.
The stoat's tail is black tipped whilst the weasel's is a uniform brown, and the stoat is generally larger. Both belie their pretty appearance by being fierce and savage hunters.
Equally active day or night, winter and summer, they are among the countryside's most common animals but their quick movements and secretive habits make them difficult to spot.
Both the hellebores (Helleborus foetidus/viridis) have a strange, other-

worldliness about them, perhaps because their distinctive green flowers appear even as the snow falls. The hellebore tends to be a woodland plant, but can thrive elsewhere and, if a mild spell of weather brings out early bees, it is one of the few nectar-bearing plants available to them in the winter months.
The frosted spider's web can be achieved by using a fine, textured thread (as opposed to plain silk) and working the web as previously described (page 53), with the addition of a seed bead in strategic places. Do not pull the threads too tightly against the background fabric – allow them to curve naturally as if pulled down by the weight of the water droplet
Embroidery shown life size:
22 x 22.5cm (8¹/₂ x 8in)

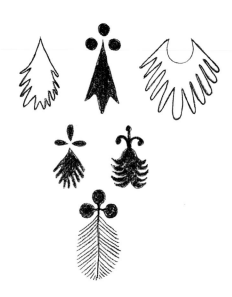

△ *Fig 54*
Heraldic 'ermines' vary considerably in their
complexity. Always depicted as a black motif on
white they would be excellent subjects on which
to practise the dalmatian-dog technique!

either by the use of a neutral grey thread for the whisker, or, as shown here, by subtly transposing black and white at the point of emergence. These tiny details may seem so minute as to be insignificant, but as we have explored throughout this book, of such is realism created. Besides, in winter the lure of the great out-doors is less and there is all the more time to consider and experiment with new techniques, develop new ideas and generally have a little fun with them.

Snow and ice and the sparkling hoarfrost of winter suggest exciting areas for experimentation. Icy ground can be conveyed through varying shades of silver, white, grey and even green. Have you ever noticed the fleeting moment when the fragile frosted crust on a cobweb begins to melt in the watery winter sun? In seconds it is over, but for an instant beads of water hang heavy from thickened, frosted gossamer.

Wrap up warmly and go for a winter walk. Explore the way in which the grasses have tangled, how the dead stems of the bindweed still cling to the black-ened arches of last year's bramble growth. In the winter the bare bones of the countryside are laid open for inspection. Store up the knowledge for next year.

FIRESIDE PROJECTS

When the harsh weather finally sets in, what could be nicer than to recall the cottage garden in early summer? Plate 69 shows just such a scene created with the use of impressionistic techniques worked on a miniature scale. The cottage itself,

PLATE 69 ▷
Miniature cottage garden
7 x 7cm (2³/4 x 2³/4in)

the grass and the path are worked in matt silk, the other features in floss. Even on such a tiny scale it is possible to suggest the identity of a number of plants. To the extreme right, tall stately hollyhocks rise on their strong stems beside the rounded shape of a rose bush, its blooms simply tiny dots of stitches. Lobelia grows low to the ground beside yellow sedum, surrounded by periwinkle and separated from another rose bush by foxgloves. Certain shrubs and fir trees have such distinctive shapes that they lend themselves well to miniaturisation whilst the country garden's main tree is worked in the same technique as the trees already discussed. The merest suggestion of a blue sky is enough to link the eye to a tiny blue reflection at the bottom right-hand corner of every window and door pane which creates the impression of glass. The cottage itself is worked initially as a type of 'etching', all the black lines creating a framework around which to build up its character. Thatch, chimney and walls are then filled in, boldly, the effect of the etching giving the building solidity and body. Refer back to Plate 8 (Introduction) to see all these techniques used with greater complexity.

A little study such as Plate 69 need not be worked from life – a summer snapshot is ideal source material. In fact many recollections of summer can serve as inspiration over the long winter months. Once when I was motoring at a leisurely pace through the Cotswolds I was intrigued to pass a five-barred gate, on which was prettily stencilled 'THE EMPRESS'. Closer inspection revealed the lady herself, contentedly munching windfalls from an adjoining orchard. The camera recorded the occasion, which could be brought to life at a later date (Plate 70).

PLATE 70 ▽

The return to traditional farming methods has seen the revival of interest in breeds of farm animals which were once almost extinct. The Gloucester Old Spot is a pig of character, still designated a 'rare breed' though steadily gaining ground. Old photographs indicate that it used to be a great deal more spotted than it now appears, though the remaining spots are well delineated. Perhaps they call for the dalmatian-pig technique?
15.5 x 8.5cm (6 x 3¼in)

Fig 55 ▷

The many and varied portraits of Queen Elizabeth I (including the famous ermine portrait) offer scope for creativity in designing miniature portraits. Go over the top with beads, sequins and feathers and create a really rich and sumptuous miniature

PLATE 71 ▷
Miniature portrait (see Fireside Projects on page 116) 5 x 7.5cm (2 x 3in)

When using photographs as design material, it is important not to be too slavish in your interpretation. If you want just an exact replica of the scene, get another print of the photo! If you want to expand your own creativity, adapt and emphasise at your own discretion. The Empress's body has been created using a single strand of stranded cotton (rather than silk). This has to be worked very closely, and the merging of the different strata must be effected as unobtrusively as possible to avoid any unnatural streaks of colour developing where the embroidery is more dense. Shading, too, is all important to create a rounded effect, and a mere suggestion of the nearby orchard and grassy paddock places the main subject in perspective.

Long winter evenings are just the time to sort through workboxes and workroom drawers, every little glory hole revealing some new discovery, long forgotten. Often a single bead, scrap of ribbon or feather can suggest a particular function, and a whole picture can evolve around it. This is what happened in the working of Plate 71. Miniature portraits (this one is only 7.5cm (3in) high, including the feather) are delightful though time-consuming projects, and each will assume its own character as it progresses. (Fig 55 is a sketch suitable for such treatment.)

The whole character of the lady in Plate 71 was suggested by her hair slide, which was in fact three tiny seed-beads which had adhered one to another in their box. The hairstyle was created to suit the slide, the hat to accommodate the hairstyle. The face is worked in a very fine split stitch, much beloved of the exponents of *Opus Anglicanum* for the working of saints' faces and hands. The medieval interpretation of the human face was stylistically rendered, with stitches often coiling to a central point on cheeks, foreheads, and so on. Here, an attempt has been made to follow the actual contour of the face and a faint blush has been added to the cheek by interspersing a pinker shade among the flesh-coloured tones. Items of jewellery have been created by the use of other seed-beads and gold thread, and the flowers of the hat are worked randomly and freehand. The tiny feather was attached at the end. Even on a tiny 'portrait' such as this, the important highlight in the eyes brings life to the figure, and further movement is suggested by the gentle curling of the hat ribbons.

NEXT SEASON'S DESIGNS

Winter can also be the time for detailed sketching and the preparation of designs for working during the following year. Plates 72 and 73 form two sections of a triptych which required very careful designing and colour matching before the work could begin. The central panel of the triptych appears in Plate 8. The theme of the work is the turning of the seasons, and the principal tree, an elm, is shown in its spring, summer and autumn aspects. The three pictures, which were ultimately mounted and framed together as a single entity, had to retain a quality of continuity. Referring only to Plates 72 and 73, apart from the changing leaf colours of the elm, each of the shrubs in the hedgerow had to develop correctly

< Fig 56
Orchids are all botanically complex, and
British varieties in particular are a challenge
to the sketcher. Shown here are (centre) the
lady's slipper and (clockwise from top right) the
butterfly orchid, bee orchid, broad-leaved
helleborine and red helleborine

PLATES 72 and 73 ▷

*Spring and autumn studies of one tree. It is
theoretically possible to produce two studies
from one sketch, but it is better to sketch the
bare bones of the tree twice. Transfer the
dimensions from one to the next for continuity's
sake and any minor differences will reflect the
tree's fortunes during the year. All trees lose the
odd branch and grow new twigs in a season.
Try 'adopting' a local tree and watch its
progress through the year; perhaps pressing
a few of its leaves at various stages for
colour reference* Both pictures
9 x 11.5cm (3¹/₂ x 4¹/₂in)

from season to season. In spring, the hawthorn was studded with sprays of white
May blossom; by autumn these bushes had to sport the showy red haws. The daf-
fodils in the right-hand foreground had disappeared completely come the autumn
and even the ivy climbing the tree trunk showed slightly darker later in the season,
and its growth had infinitesimally progressed. Scattered autumn leaves replaced
the other yellow and pink flowers of spring. Beyond the now golden, harvested
field in the autumn study the sky is tinged pink with sunset, whilst in the spring
variant a pale rain-washed blue is suggested.

For detailed studies such as these it may be useful to colour your sketches.
This need not be done with any great precision (indeed the loose sketching of
leaves on tree and hedgerow would not allow a detailed 'painting by numbers'
approach) but a gentle watercolour wash indicating some of the more atmospheric
shades may well be helpful, especially if you do not anticipate starting the embroidery immediately.

An anatomically and botanically correct study such as Plate 74 also requires a
great deal of patient research and planning before it can be undertaken realistically.

The scale of the component parts, their positioning and, most importantly, their colour matching (given the immensely complex plumage of the bird) all require careful planning. If you do not have all the information required in your own collection of books, a quiet afternoon in the warmth of the local library, or even a trip to the Natural History Museum can be a worthwhile investment of your time.

BACK TO REALITY

In the New Year, even as the days begin to lengthen, winter still appears to hold the countryside in an icy grip, yet some wildflowers bloom throughout these bleak days, and others push through the snow to remind us that spring is indeed coming. February can be the coldest month of the year but the study in Plate 75 shows flowers seen blooming on St Valentine's Day, 14 February. Warm breath condensed in the cold air, but already the pretty male catkins of the hazel were dropping their pollen and the heady fragrance of the sweet violets was as welcome as

△ *Fig 57*
Hothouse orchids can be particularly effective on a black background, where voiding comes into play. Top and left are cymbidium, *bottom right* cypripedium reginae, *not dissimilar to the wild lady's slipper orchid*

PLATE 74 ▽

The green woodpecker (Picus viridis) *goes by
the old country name of the yaffle, a reference to
its loud, laughing call. It is not uncommon in
gardens and active in the winter, when it may
well be attracted to bird tables, much to the
chagrin of smaller birds. As an insect feeder, it
often searches for food on the ground (unlike
other woodpeckers) and has also been known to*
disturb wild bee colonies in search of their
grubs. The yaffle's plumage incorporates almost
every type of feather work we have explored:
ticking on the head and cheek; individual
feathers; overlaying and dalmatian-dog
spotting; and broad banding on the tail.
Unusually in British birds, it also has a blue
eye, giving it a distinctive character.
Bee orchids (Ophrys apifera) *have evolved
specifically to attract bees for the purpose of
pollination. In their colouring and shape they
ape both the mining bee and the larger red-*
tailed bumble bee (Bombus lapidarius) *shown
here. The incredible complexity of an orchid's
flower must never tempt the would-be
naturalist to pick a specimen for closer study.
Although certain species are gaining ground this
is entirely due to the protection and
conservation now afforded them. Study
photographs and good botanical plates
(Victorian prints are excellent) to begin an
understanding of orchid anatomy*
Embroidery shown life size:
26 x 18cm (10¼ x 7in)

◁ *Fig 58*
Even the names of many wayside plants invite
one into the embroiderer's countryside.
Lady's smock and shepherd's needle
symbolise the alliance

kisses after a long separation. The dancing ballet skirts of the snowdrops bobbed between tiny flowers of sapphire blue and snowflake white. The long winter has its own beauty, sweet with anticipation of the year to come.

We have explored the embroiderer's countryside in all its seasons, but hardly in all its moods and certainly not in all its diversity, though by now we can approach these Valentine's Day flowers without too much trepidation. We know how to capture the lightness of their movement, how to catch for a fleeting moment the flickering shadows thrown by the winter sun, how sweeping stitches will describe petal and leaf and how a sinuous stem can curve and coil and bind the attention. As the seasons pass, fresh seeds of inspiration will be sown, new challenges will emerge and techniques will evolve to hold them fast to the fabric. Growth of seedling and sapling will be reflected through stitch and silk for as long as the countryside endures.

PLATE 75 ST VALENTINE'S DAY
*Was there ever a more apt description than
'lambs' tails' for the male catkins of the hazel
(*Corylus avellana*)? The snowdrop
(*Galanthus nivalis*) and the fragrant sweet
violet (*Viola odorata*) are also aptly named.
The common field speedwell (*Veronica
persica*) flowers freely throughout the year, as
does the common chickweed (*Stellaria media*).
The chickweed is so ethereal that shadowing the
bright-green leaves would destroy their lively
spontaneity: proof that every rule is there to be
broken* Embroidery shown life size:
28.5 x 18cm (11^{1}/$_{4}$ x 7in)

HELEN
STEVENS

APPENDIX

the practicalities

working conditions and equipment

○ LIGHTING

The first prerequisite is good lighting. Without this, not only will the work itself become trying, but identifying colours becomes almost impossible. Daylight is the finest and most natural light of all, especially when dealing with natural history subjects, and working in the open air or in a window seat can be the most enjoyable and relaxing of pastimes.

If daylight is not available or not sufficient a good spotlight is a worthwhile investment. Models with dual wattage allow a choice of high or low level of spotlighting which is especially useful when using metallic threads, as a very bright light on gold and silver threads can sometimes dazzle.

Always work with the spotlight in the same position in relation to your embroidery, so that you become familiar with the angle of the light. Any shadow cast by your hand will soon become unnoticeable. Obviously, keep the light in such a position that any shadow will not cut across the stitching.

If you are working on a fine fabric, avoid having a high level of light immediately behind the work, as this will have the effect of making the fabric transparent, and can be very distracting. If you are working outdoors keep the sun behind you, but wear a hat or use a sun shade, as concentration plus sunlight can lead to headaches and eyestrain.

○ EMBROIDERY FRAMES

In fine flat embroidery the tension of the background fabric is all important and it is essential to work on an embroidery frame. Round 'tambour' frames, so called because they resemble a tambourine, are best suited to fine work, as the tension they produce is entirely uniform. These frames are available in a large range of sizes, from 8-10cm (3-4in) in diameter to large, free-standing models 60-65cm (24-26in) in diameter. The choice of size

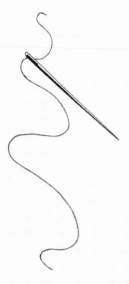

will depend upon the subject matter and size of the embroidery to be worked. Clearly, it is wasteful of fabric to use a frame much larger than is needed (always allowing for sufficient fabric around the design to mount the picture), but there are occasions when a larger than expected frame should be used. A freestanding frame is especially useful when techniques such as couching are to be included in the work, as these require two hands.

Tambour frames are available in a range of materials, including plastic, but it is still hard to improve upon the traditional wooden frame. Those with keys which adjust the tightness of fit between inner and outer frame are useful, but with a little practice the ancient design of two hoops which fit firmly yet smoothly together without the aid of any mechanical device can be mastered (and it is a fascinating thought that this type of hoop frame has been in use unchanged for thousands of years).

Whichever frame is chosen it is essential that it should feel comfortable to use. If the diameter is more than approximately 35cm (14in) it can become too heavy, when dressed, to be hand held without making the arm tired, so it should therefore be freestanding. Ideally, a hand-held tambour frame should be small enough for the fingers of the hand in which it is held to reach from the outer rim to the centre of the frame without straining, as they will be able to guide the needle when it is on the reverse of the fabric. This is a general rule which depends on the size of the worker's hand, but it is a good guide. Freestanding frames, frames which include a support which can be held beneath the leg when seated, and frames held in a vice should be at a level which allows the worker to sit comfortably and work without strain. Again, a good rule of thumb is that the embroiderer should be able to reach to the centre of the dressed frame without stretching unduly when the elbow is at the level of the outer rim.

If the design fills a large proportion of the stretched fabric it is sometimes necessary to turn the frame upside down whilst working. With a little practice this is no problem, but remember to reorientate any 'imagined light source' which is being embroidered as part of the overall scheme.

○ OTHER EQUIPMENT

The choice of smaller tools is a personal one. Embroidery scissors must be small, fine and sharp, whatever their design. The finer your choice of threads, the sharper and keener the scissors must be – the very finest silk can slip unharmed through a dull or

Fig a ▷
With the thumb on the outer ring of the tambour frame, the fingers of the hand should just be able to reach the centre of the circle. Similarly, with a larger frame, with the elbow at the ring, the fingers should reach the centre

loose pair of scissors which seem quite adequate when used upon cotton or wool!

Needles, too, must be chosen with the specific use of threads and fabric in mind. It is a good idea to have a selection of various sizes to avoid frustration when a new piece of work is begun. Sizes 5 to 10 are generally the most useful. The eye of the needle should accept the thread easily, but not too loosely, and the needle should pull the thread smoothly through the chosen fabric. If it has to be tugged through the stretched material (with a resulting 'thunk' as the material acts like the skin of a drum) you have picked the wrong needle for the job. The thread fragments in the needle and the constant strain will make the fabric loose and floppy within the frame – and spell disaster!

For metallic threads use either a wide-eyed embroidery needle or a crewel needle of suitable size, depending on the technique. A substantial gold or silver thread, when couched, will lie wholly on the surface of the work and will not need to be threaded at all. When using metallic threads take care that the needle does not become dull through constant contact with the metal.

The use of a thimble is a matter for personal choice. I find that a thimble dulls my sense of touch and therefore hinders delicate or fine work, though it can be useful when couching. If you use a thimble, be sure that it fits snugly and be careful that it has no worn or jagged edges which may catch in the work – this applies to all the tools discussed.

materials

In any form of embroidery, the look of the finished work will depend not only upon the skill of the artist, but also upon the choice of fabric and thread. There are no 'right' or 'wrong' choices when it comes to making these decisions and, so long as certain practical considerations are borne in mind, the intuitive inspiration of the embroiderer is as important in this sphere as it is in the choice of subject matter.

For so-called flat-work embroidery which must be worked in a frame, it is essential that the fabric chosen for the background does not stretch. If it stretches even slightly while embroidery is in progress, when removed from the frame it will contract to its normal size, and the embroidery will be distorted. Any fabric with no stretch is a possible choice, but, unless you have a specific desire for a textured background, it is also a good idea to look for a smooth fabric.

The pictures in this book have been worked upon an inexpensive cotton/polyester fabric (sometimes called 'percale') which is very lightweight. Poly-cotton mixes (preferably even-weave) in a heavier weight are also ideal for use in this type of embroidery. Larger pictures should be worked on heavier fabrics, smaller studies on lightweights, but this rule can be adapted to the particular needs of the picture in question.

Try to avoid fabrics with too loose a weave, as too many stitches will be vying for space in too few threads of warp and weft and the result will be unsatisfactory. Pure cotton and linen

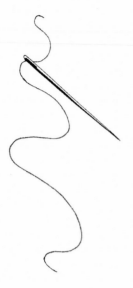

evenweaves are also ideal, but as a general rule for this type of 'freestyle' embroidery, if the weave is open enough to be used for counted thread embroidery it is too wide for us! Percale and other poly-cotton mixes are available in a range of colours from most dressmaking and haberdashery stores.

The choice of threads depends upon a number of factors. Although most of the pictures in this book are worked in pure silk, other fibres are quite suitable and might prove more practicable for beginners. Stranded cottons, which have been used in some of the work featured, are adaptable and widely available in a large range of colours. When split down into single threads they can be delicate enough to convey all but the finest details, and are fine enough to allow themselves to be 'mixed' in the needle. Avoid those skeins which vary their shades throughout their length. They may seem like a time-saving way to graduate your colours but they are rarely convincing. It is better to re-thread your needle several times with slightly different shades. Shiny rayons and nylons can also be attractive, but their colours may not be as natural as you could wish, so choose carefully.

Pure silk threads are, of course, the finest and most enjoyable to use, though their behaviour in the needle can be frustrating to beginners. There are many different types of silk thread to choose from (and now an increasing choice of manufacturers), so it is well to decide upon the desired effect before spending too much on a large selection.

Most of the pictures featured in this book are worked with the equivalent of 'floss' silks, which are untwisted and therefore very shiny. The advantage of using floss is that it can be split down into very fine strands for the minutest detailed work, and then used doubled, or even trebled, to describe the more substantial parts of the design. For this reason it is ideal when it comes to 'mixing' colours in the needle. An almost infinite variety of shades can be achieved, which is particularly important for natural history subjects. The disadvantages of floss is that by virtue of its untwisted state it can fragment in the needle during the course of working, and, especially if you have rough skin, can catch, fray and generally become very irritating! One solution to this problem is to make sure that your hands remain as smooth and soft as possible, and remember that a rough fingernail (or any other jagged edge) can damage your work almost beyond repair if it catches in embroidery already in situ. There are hand creams available to help keep your skin in perfect condition for silkwork. Make sure that you do not use a cream which leaves the skin greasy or sticky as this may leave marks on your fabric and 'pollute' the silk itself. Working with floss silk is a gentle time-consuming art and it may well affect other aspects of your life!

Twisted silks are slightly easier to work with and also have a glorious shine. If they are not twisted too tightly, they may be split down into finer strands for detailed work, and then used in their original state for covering large areas. They are also useful in combination with floss silks to describe areas which do not require such a high level of sheen, for instance, buildings, roads and other man-made aspects of country life.

Stranded silks are a fairly recent innovation. These are a great boon to anyone used to stranded cottons, as they are in similar format and may be used either split into single threads or as up to six strands together. They are flexible, easy to use, come in a delightful range of colours and are altogether recommended as having the best elements of both floss and twisted silk.

Some years ago it was almost impossible to buy pure silk for embroidery, as most manufacturers gave up production when fashions turned toward synthetics. Happily this trend is now reversing, but there is still much enjoyment to be had searching for second-hand silks. Jumble sales, bygone fairs and 'trash and treasure' events are all prime hunting grounds where you may find an old workbox from thirty or forty years ago, with its precious contents intact – if extensively tangled. There is magic to be found in the use of pre-war silks, and colours long deleted from manufacturers' shade cards can be a very useful addition to your palette.

As you become more adventurous and increasingly involved with your embroideries, you will acquire a vast selection of colours as each new project will undoubtedly require one or two new shades to be added to your collection. However, initially you will need to buy a range of universally useful colours which will adapt themselves to your preferred subject matter. Rather than acquiring a huge range of bright,

unconnected colours, many of which will lie untouched in your workbox for years, it is better to decide upon about six basics and get up to three shades of each. For instance, green is obviously a prerequisite of any countryside embroidery project, so buy a true mid-toned green, together with a paler version of the same colour and a darker one for shadowing, etc. Similarly with browns, a fine earthy brown should be complemented by a pale gold and a dark donkey brown. Apply the same principle to pinks, blues, yellow/orange and lilac and you will have a fine basic palette to begin an interpretation of the countryside. Needless to say, white and black are also essentials.

The choice of metallic thread is wide and varied. It is very difficult to find real gold and silver thread (and extremely expensive) and with so many good synthetics on the market it would seem pedantic to insist – though some are featured in the illustrations. Jap gold is usually manufactured in too loose a format to be effective for very fine couching, but passing thread is ideal for most of the jobs described. Stranded gold and silver are also available for the finest work, but with so many options, the best advice is simply to plan an excursion to a good needlework shop and have fun choosing for yourself!

Finally, of course, there are all the little extras which make collecting threads and materials more than a practical job and take it into the realms of fantasy. Specialist threads, tiny seed pearls and beads, and the occasional sequin and feather all deserve a place in some secret little glory-hole at the

back of your workbox. Planning for their use in advance is usually hopeless – you will know when you see them that they will 'come in handy one day' and they will!

translating your sketches

Whether you are working from your own sketch, from a design suggested by the drawings in this book, or from a photograph or pre-prepared design, the first step is to transfer the pattern from paper to fabric. It is important to remember that every line which is transferred onto your background fabric is there permanently, and must therefore be covered by embroidery. Very fine details should be omitted from the transfer process, as fine embroidery would not be heavy enough to disguise the transferred line. Such fine detail must be worked free-hand at a later date.

For transferring a design to fabric you will need:
- Tracing paper
- Large piece of firm cardboard (or wooden drawing board)
- Straight pins (drawing pins)
- Dull pencil, or other stylus
- Ruler
- Dressmaker's carbon paper (dressmaker's tracing paper)
- Flat, smooth table
- Background fabric (see page 127 for fabrics) (Remember to leave a large border around your work for mounting.)

Tracing paper is available in various weights. A good weight is approximately 90gsm, but you may need to undertake a little trial and error before you find the right weight for your chosen fabric.

DO NOT be tempted to use a typewriter carbon paper. The carbon will rub off on the fabric and is very difficult to remove. Dressmaker's carbon paper (or dressmaker's tracing paper) which is available in most fabric and embroidery stores and haberdashery departments is designed specifically for our purposes. It is usually to be bought in packets of assorted colours and has a hard, waxy finish.

Fig b ▷

When planning your design, you might like to use the classical 'perfect dimension' of 16:9, on which the Parthenon was based. Seen empty, the resulting rectangle seems elongated, but the dimension becomes easily filled and is strangely harmonious to the human eye. It can be used landscape or portrait

° METHOD

1 Make a tracing of the chosen design. Place a sheet of tracing paper (this may have to be cut to size) over the pattern and carefully draw over each line with a lead pencil. In any large areas of the design which will be entirely covered by embroidery, you may wish to indicate the direction of stitching by shading. Check that you have traced all the required information (minus fine detail) before removing the paper from the design.

2 Place the cardboard on a flat surface, and lay your fabric out on it. If you use a wooden drawing board make sure that it is padded with several sheets of lining paper as this is necessary to produce a smooth, even line. Carefully position the traced design over the fabric, making sure that the 'north/south' alignment of the design is in line with the weave of the fabric. If the design is to be centred, use a ruler to find the mid point. Pin the design to the fabric and into the board at the four corners, using the drawing pins.

Do not forget the importance of leaving a good sized border around your work, for effect as well as mounting. Your design may suddenly look very small on a large expanse of fabric, but this is only an illusion.

3 Choose a sheet of carbon paper in a colour which contrasts with your fabric. (White 'chalked' carbon paper will rub off as work progresses, so beginners may prefer to use the more waxy yellow or orange carbon paper on dark fabrics.)

Slip the carbon, colour side down,

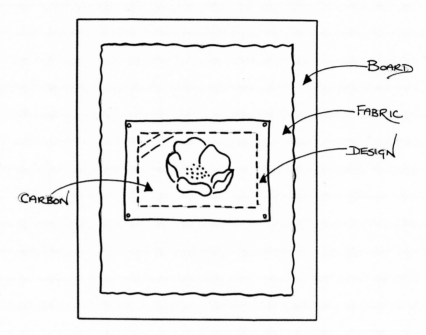

between the tracing and the fabric, removing one of the corner pins to do so. Replace the pin. Do not pin through the carbon paper. Using your pencil (by now your pencil should be dull, as a sharp pencil applying a hard pressure to the tracing paper will damage it) trace a few lines of the design. Remove one of the pins, raise one corner of the tracing and the carbon and check the impression. If the result is too heavy, apply slightly less pressure, if it is too light, a little more pressure. Replace the sheets and the pin and trace the whole of the design through onto the fabric. Take care not to smudge the carbon by resting your hand on top of the tracing while working, and do not let the pencil mark the fabric.

4 Remove the carbon and all but two of the top pins and check that all the design is transferred before removing the tracing.

Fig c △
The carbon paper, shown partly hatched, is interleaved carefully between the background fabric and the design paper

○ PREPARING THE EMBROIDERY

There are various methods of 'dressing' a tambour frame. The procedure set out below has the advantage of not adding any weight to a hand-held frame and it may be used on all types and sizes of tambour frames.

1　Lay the inner ring of the tambour on a flat, clean surface.

2　Over this, place a sheet of tissue paper. If a large frame is used (ie larger than the individual sheets of paper) cut the tissue into wide strips and stick them loosely to the ring using double-sided sticky tape.

3　Position the fabric over this, and put a second sheet of tissue paper over both. If a large frame is used, cut wide strips of the paper and lay them around the edges of the work.

4　Position the outer ring of the frame over the whole ensemble and press down smoothly but firmly. If using a keyed frame, tighten the screw to the appropriate tension.

5　Cut away the tissue paper to reveal the design beneath. Turn the frame over and cut away the tissue paper at the back to reveal the underside of the work. The remaining paper will protect the edges and avoid leaving a 'ring' around your finished work.

At all times when not in use your frame and its precious contents should be covered and kept clean. Work on pale fabric, in particular, is vulnerable to the least speck of dirt. Always wash your hands before beginning to embroider and throw a cover over your frame if you leave it unattended – particularly if you are working outdoors!

presentation

○ MOUNTING

For mounting, you will need:
- Hardboard (or very stiff cardboard) cut to the size of the finished work (Remember to make this big enough for the framing, and smooth off the edges thoroughly.)

Fig d ▽

The tissue paper lies on top of the fabric, the upper ring of the frame ready to hold the two together. The design would be hidden beneath the tissue at this stage; it is shown here to indicate its position within the frame

Fig e ▽

Once mated with its lower counterpart, the frame becomes whole, sandwiching two layers of tissue and the fabric. The tissue is then cut away top and bottom to reveal the design, and conveniently trimmed around the outside of the ring for ease of handling

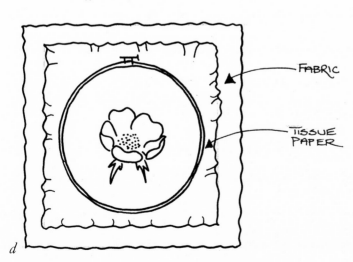

FABRIC

TISSUE PAPER

d

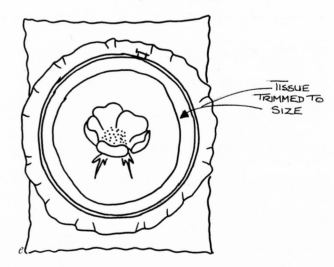

TISSUE TRIMMED TO SIZE

e

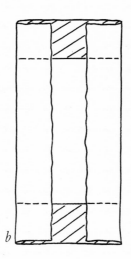
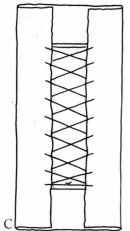
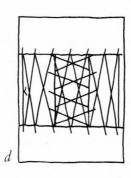

◁ *Fig f*
Mounting the embroidery:
'a' Embroidery is placed face down, backing
board positioned on top
'b' The outer sides of the fabric are folded in
'c' They are laced, corset fashion
'd' The top and bottom edges of the fabric are
treated similarly

- Acid-free cartridge paper cut to the same size, white for work on a pale ground, black for work on black
- Clear sticky tape
- Fabric scissors
- Two large-eyed needles
- Lacing thread (mercerised cotton, or similar thread which will not stretch)
- Iron and ironing board

○ METHOD

1   Press the embroidery on the wrong side, without steam (after checking the manufacturer's instructions for fabric and thread).

2   Using a small amount of sticky tape, secure the cartridge paper to the surface of the board.

3   Position the embroidery right side up over the covered board, and, leaving a margin of at least 4cm (1½in) cut the fabric to size. Leave a larger margin for larger pieces of work or for heavy fabric.

4   Carefully, and without shifting the position of the embroidery in relation to the board, turn the whole ensemble over so that the embroidery is face

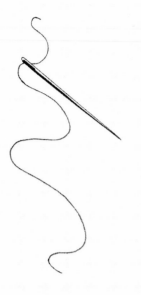

down, and the board on top of it. Make sure you are working on a clean surface.

5 Cut a long but manageable piece of lacing thread, and thread a needle at each end of the thread, with two 'tails' of similar length.

6 Fold the two sides of the fabric to the centre of the board.

7 Working from the top, insert a needle on either side and lace the two sides of the fabric together corset fashion until you reach the bottom. If you run out of lacing thread, simply tie the thread off and begin again with more thread.

8 Fold the top and bottom of the fabric towards the centre and repeat the lacing process. It takes a little practice to achieve perfect tension. Do not over-tighten the laces as they may break, or rip the fabric, but do not be afraid of creating a reasonable pull on the work as only in this way will the original tension of the fabric on the tambour be re-created. Always tie off the ends of the lacing thread with firm, non-slip knots, and snip off any extra thread which is left.

○ FRAMING

The choice of frame is a personal matter, but always be prepared to take professional advice, as framing can make or mar a picture. On a practical level, the rebate on any frame must be deep enough to accommodate the mounted work, the window mount required to lift the glass from the work (essential if small beads, etc have been used), the glass and a sheet of cardboard holding the entire ensemble together. This may limit your choice, but a good professional framer will have a wide enough selection of mouldings.

Arguments concerning the respective advantages and otherwise of non-reflective glass have raged for so long that this, too, must be left to individual preference, though I feel that non-reflective glass lessens the sharpness of the work, and to some extent tends to dull the colours. No room is so clean and free of dust that it is safe to leave fine silk-work unprotected by glass, and the temptation to touch, must at all cost be prevented.

Avoid hanging work immediately above radiators or fireplaces, as exposure to concentrated dry heat may warp frame and contents. Bathrooms and kitchens are obvious areas to avoid. No picture should be hung in direct prolonged sunlight. However, to be seen to their best advantage, embroideries need a good level of lighting and ordinary daylight will do little harm. A small spotlight positioned so that it illuminates the work from above will bring it to life, especially in the evenings. Take a little time to achieve the most effective angle of lighting.

Imaginatively framed and with sympathetic lighting, even a small embroidery can provide a focal point. Conversation will naturally turn to its working, and its subject matter, and that in turn may also be of some benefit to the greater environment.

ACKNOWLEDGEMENTS

No book is written in a vacuum, and this one would not have seen the light of day without the help and encouragement of many friends too numerous to mention who have helped me retain my sanity – they know who they are!

Special thanks, too, for the professional help and personal encouragement from all those involved in the preparation of manuscript and photographs, in particular Nigel and Angela Salmon, Sheila Haman, Brenda Sortwell (for her invaluable advice on materials, etc) Robin Hart for information on folk customs and, of course, Vivienne Wells for getting the project off the ground and guiding me through the pitfalls.

And to my many patient clients, who have allowed their own pictures to be reproduced in this book – I could not have done it without you! Plates 1 and 61, courtesy of Mr and Mrs D. Godson; Plates 2, 35, 10 and 75, Cdr and Mrs M. A. Tibby; Plate 3, Mrs J. Fuller; Plates 4 and 60, Mrs D. Leach; Plate 5, Mrs A. Kelly; Plate 6, Mrs L. Paites; Plate 7, Mr A. Way; Plates 8, 72 and 73, Mrs D. Anstead; Plate 12, Mrs V. Pether; Plates 14 and 34, Mrs M. Cooper; Plates 15 and 51, Mrs J. Precious; Plates 20, 37 and 40, Mr and Mrs A. W. Cooper; Plate 21, Hazel Fletcher; Plate 22, Mrs P. Ashman; Plate 25, Miss N. Applegate; Plate 26, Mrs J. M. Tarplett; Plates 28 and 29, Mrs D. Poole; Plate 30, Mrs J. Allen; Plates 33 and 63, Mr and Mrs G. Rous; Plate 34, Mr J. Precious; Plates 36, 38 and 65, Mrs M. Hide; Plate 41, Mrs J. Stratton; Plate 42, Mr and Mrs B. J. W. Miller; Plate 44, Mrs J. Brown; Plate 45, Mr P. J. Leeder; Plates 47 and 48, Mrs M. E. Baker; Plate 49, Mr and Mrs J. B. Deering; Plate 50, Mrs B. O'Carroll; Plate 52, Miss L. Webber; Plate 53, Mrs J. Bruce; Plate 56, Mrs M. Dicken; Plates 58 and 59, Mr and Mrs P. R. Williams; Plate 66, Mr and Mrs R. Abraham; Plate 69, Mrs E. M. Ling; Plate 70, Mr D. Hale; Plate 71, Mrs J. Atkinson; Plate 74, Mrs Olive Bacon.

INDEX